the best of FAIZ

the best of **FAIZ**

translated by SHIV K. KUMAR

PENGUIN BOOKS
An imprint of Penguin Random House

PENGUIN BOOKS

USA | Canada | UK | Ireland | Australia
New Zealand | India | South Africa | China | Singapore

Penguin Books is part of the Penguin Random House group of companies whose addresses can be found at global.penguinrandomhouse.com

Published by Penguin Random House India Pvt. Ltd
4th Floor, Capital Tower 1, MG Road,
Gurugram 122 002, Haryana, India

Penguin Random House India

First published by Random House India 2013
This edition published in Penguin Books by Penguin Random House India 2020

10 9 8 7 6 5 4 3 2

ISBN 9788184003826

Typeset in Adobe Garamond by R. Ajith Kumar
Printed at Manipal Technologies Limited, India

www.penguin.co.in

FSC www.fsc.org MIX Paper | Supporting responsible forestry FSC® C043100

This is a legitimate digitally printed version of the book and therefore might not have certain extra finishing on the cover.

For
Sharad Dutt—
One of the best things
that ever happened to me

Contents

Dast-é-Saba

Foreword

Poet, journalist, translator, film-maker, broadcaster, Marxist and recipient of the Lenin Peace Prize, Faiz Ahmed Faiz grew into a legend in his lifetime. When he died on 20 November 1984, his admirers all over the world felt that a literary era had come to an end.

I first met him in 1979 when he came to Hyderabad. I was asked to preside over one of his poetry readings, while introducing him to the audience, in what turned out to be my first ever public speech in Urdu, I said, 'Ye rahe Faiz Sahib—hum watan, hum zabaan aur hum pasha . . .' This was because we were both natives of Lahore (a city he loved, although he was born in Sialkot); we shared the same mother tongue (Punjabi); and we had both started our careers as lecturers in English. But what I now cherish is the memory of an evening with him in Hyderabad. When I told him how his poetry had influenced mine, although I wrote in English, he responded modestly that he had been unjustifiably overrated, and that he was only too conscious of his limitations. There lay the secret of his charisma—his humility, which is so rare in most contemporary writers. I then told him that while, as Professor of English, I lectured on British and American poetry, it was in his poetry, Iqbal's or Ghalib's, that I sought sustenance for my soul. To this he responded, with a dimpled smile: 'It's the mystique of Urdu words, I guess, that does it. Hasn't Urdu its unique aura of sound and meaning? . . . Also, it carries an emotional charge of such high voltage as is not found in most Western poetry.'

A Rebel

An irrepressible rebel, Faiz never submitted himself to any form of tyranny—political, social or religious. As a poet-thinker, he believed that art should not be divorced from social reality. This commitment to social and political justice was accentuated by the long spells of incarceration he had to undergo. Prison, therefore, emerges in his poetry as a predominant metaphor that embodies his poetic vision.

All his life, he waged a relentless struggle as poet, journalist and activist, for the emancipation of the common man from injustice and oppression.

A truly enlightened government, he believed, must be dedicated to the welfare of the daily wage-earner. No wonder, when Pakistan achieved independence, he felt anguished to see the so-called political liberators as only neo-colonials, drunk on power. This disillusionment is the theme of his poem titled 'The Morning of Freedom, August 1947':

> . . . this is not the morning we'd fought for,
> in whose eager quest, all comrades
> had set out, hoping that somewhere
> in the wilderness of the sky
> would emerge the ultimate destination of stars . . .

But while he lamented that his country's independence brought no relief to the daily wage-earner, he knew that the new political overlords could not muzzle the common man's urge for social and political justice. In one of his moving poems,

'Dogs', symbolizing the labour classes, he warns that if denied their rights, they could shake up the pillars of power. Like 'The Man with the Hoe', in Edward Markham's poem, the labourer would some day 'rise like a dumb terror to judge the world'. So let not these street dogs be kept under perpetual tyranny, for

> If these destitutes ever stirred up . . .
> . . . they could chew up even the bones of their
> masters.

> All this—
> if only someone would awaken them to their ignominy,
> shake their sagging tails
> to action.

But in spite of a Marxist undercurrent in his poetry, Faiz remained, essentially, a romantic poet—impelled by his passion for his beloved—the theme that dominates most Urdu poetry. This dilemma between Marxist thought and romantic love is incisively resolved in his poem 'Poesy's Domain'. While recognizing the validity of such themes as hunger and social justice, Faiz turns to the muse's perennial preoccupation—love.

> These luscious corn-fields bursting with youth
> why do they yield hunger alone?
> All these themes are there indeed—and many more
> but the gently parting lips of that beauty,
> and, oh, the alluring contours of her body
> now tell me yourself, could there be such witchery
> elsewhere?

Well, for me, this is it—
a poet's mental province can be none other than this.

It would, therefore, be appropriate to say that Faiz's all-embracing poetic vision is like a mighty river that carries in its sweep countless tributaries. Faiz denies no experience, excludes nothing, to project reality in all its baffling complexity. He is a poet of many moods, and his work is a mosaic of diverse concerns—of classicism and modernity, of political commitment and romantic love, of affirmation and denial.

A Poet in Exile

Faiz travelled extensively abroad, in the USA, England and the Middle East. But wherever he went, he yearned for Pakistan, 'my other Laila, my land'. To quote from his poem 'Two Loves' ('Do Ishq'):

Just so have I craved for
My other Laila, my land.
So has my heart fluttered
With the same longing.

Celebrated literary orientalist, Edward Said, describes his meeting with Faiz, in Beirut. 'To see a poet in exile, as opposed to reading his poetry of exile—is to see exile's antinomies embodied and endured . . . Several years ago, I spent some time with Faiz Ahmed Faiz, the greatest of contemporary Urdu poets . . .'

Besides being a widely travelled man, Faiz had also read extensively in Western literature, particularly Latin American. So he could look at the Western man from an oriental point of view, and the oriental man from the Western standpoint. It is this bifocal vision that lends a new dimension to his well-known poem 'Paris'. To him, the West is a wasteland of emotional sterility, of loneliness and an innate incapacity for genuine emotion. To the Western man, like Eliot's carbuncular lover, sex is a mere biological function.

Music of Words

The poetry of Faiz embodies the music of words. In a note on his boyhood and youth, he recalls how he was introduced to classical music by his friend Khwaja Khurshid Anwar, who was a member of the revolutionary group led by Bhagat Singh. This may explain Faiz's unique sense of rhythm, cadence, assonance and resonance. Of all the senses he evokes, the auditory is the most conspicuous. Even when his lines don't rhyme, as in his poem 'Yaad' ('Remembrance'), any reader endowed with auditory imagination may 'hear' the reverberations of music that flows through it:

> In the wilderness of my heart, O love,
> waver
> the shadows of your voice
> the mirages of your lips . . .

No wonder, his poetry lends itself so readily to such ghazal singers as Iqbal Bano, Begum Akhtar, Mehdi Hasan and Noor Jehan. His language is multiversant; he can move effortlessly from formal prose syntax to freewheeling structures. After all, 'a poet', he once remarked to a fellow Pakistani writer, 'is not a grammarian or a lexicographer. Language is his tool, the material he uses to create. It is thus subservient to him, not he to it.'

Synthesis of Tradition and Modernity

This brings me to another aspect of his poetry—is it classical or modern? While some critics consider him a traditionalist, others applaud him as an innovator. In fact, his poetry is a creative synthesis of both tradition and experiment. If he uses such traditional images as the caravan, the night of union or separation, the dawn of hope, etc., he never fails to alchemize each such image so as to invest it with a new meaning and coherence. In fact, his unique achievement, according to Edward Said, 'was to have created a contrapuntal rhetoric and rhythm whereby he could use classical forms (qasida, ghazal, masnavi) and transform them before his reader rather than break away from the old forms . . . The critical thing to understand about Faiz is that like Garcia Marquez, he was read and listened to both by the literary elite and by the masses.'

As a Humanist

Faiz may be called a citizen of the world because he felt at home everywhere, be it Paris, Chicago, London or Beirut.

Since he was a liberal humanist, he considered all human beings members of a global family. Islam, to him, was synonymous with peace and love. True religion, according to him, is a unifying force; it does not generate differences between one community and another. So Faiz was adored and admired both in Pakistan and India. If he were alive today, he would have certainly advocated open borders between all countries of the Indian subcontinent—India, Pakistan, Bangladesh, Myanmar and Sri Lanka.

One wonders how Faiz would have reacted to religious extremism, which has become the scourge of our time. His humanism would have abhorred places of worship being used as centres of terror. He would have said with Iqbal, his favourite poet, that *mazhab nahin sikhata apas mein beir rakhna.* (Religion does not teach us to nourish hatred for one another.)

Creation and Criticism

If Faiz often refrained from responding to professional critics, it was because he believed that poetic process was autotelic. In his introductory note to *Naqsh-e-Faryadi*, he says, 'So whenever these literary sleuths ask me why I write poetry, I often say anything that comes to my mind, just to put them off.'

Critics, he thought, exulted in long-winded commentaries, without savouring life itself. They are like someone who stands on the bank of a river, taking it as his ultimate destination, while the poet plunges into deep waters, for isn't that the only way to taste the flavour of the water in midstream?

Tum dur khade dekha hi kiye
Aur doobne wala doob gaya
Tum sahil ko manzil samjhe
Tum lazzaté darya kya jano

In any case, Faiz believed that creation and criticism are co-extensive, for doesn't a poet function as his own critic while revising his work—expunging, modifying, adding, etc. So why should one create an arbitrary hiatus between a poet's creative and critical faculties?

Only once did Faiz open up to say that there was no fixed pattern in his mode of writing. Often while listening to music, a specific note or a certain rhythmic form, would send him off to writing. Or it could be a line, a phrase, or an image from a book he was reading . . . or, an exciting event, a sudden encounter with a stranger—in fact, anything anywhere could stir his imagination. While a ghazal, according to Faiz, emerges from a rhyming scheme in the poet's mind, a nazm demands deliberation.

It is difficult to sum up a poet like Faiz, whose multi-splendoured genius encompasses human experience in its entirety—mind, body and soul. I earnestly believe that, after Mir, Ghalib and Iqbal, he should be recognized as the greatest Urdu poet.

Shiv K. Kumar

Poems

सुरूदे शबाना

नीम शब चाँद खुद फ़रामोशी
महफ़िले हस्तो-बूद वीराँ है
पैकरे इल्तेजा है ख़ामोशी
बज़्मे अंजुम फसुर्दा सामाँ है
आबशारे सुकूत जारी है
चार सू बेखुदी सी तारी है
ज़िन्दगी जुज़्वे ख़्वाब है गोया
सारी दुनिया सराब है गोया

सो रही है घने दरख़्तों पर
चाँदनी की थकी हुई आवाज़
कहकशाँ नीमवा निगाहों से
कह रही है हदीसे शौक़े नयाज़
साज़े दिल के ख़मोश तारों से
छन रहा है खुमारे कैफ़ आगीं
आरज़ू, ख़्वाब, तेरा रूए हसीं

سرودِ شبانہ

نیم شب‘ چاند‘ خود فراموشی
محفلِ ہست و بود ویراں ہے
پیکرِ التجا ہے خاموشی
بزمِ انجم فسردہ ساماں ہے
آبشارِ سکوت جاری ہے
چار سُو بے خودی سی طاری ہے
زندگی جزوِ خواب ہے گویا
ساری دنیا سَراب ہے گویا

سو رہی ہے گھنے درختوں پر !
چاندنی کی تھکی ہوئی آواز
کہکشاں نیم وا نگاہوں سے
کہہ رہی ہے حدیثِ شوقِ نیاز
سازِ دل کے خموش تاروں سے
چھن رہا ہے خمارِ کیف آگیں
آرزو‘ خواب‘ تیرا رُوئے حسیں

The Melody of Night

Midnight, moon, self-forgetfulness—
desolate is the theatre of being.
Silence is desire incarnate
and sad the conclave of stars.
This ceaseless cataract of tranquillity—
oblivion reigns all around
as though existence is a mere fragment of a dream
and the entire world a mirage.

On the clustered treetops,
the jaded cry of moonlight sleeps.
With half-shut eyes, the constellations
seem to articulate my humble payer to you.
Through the mute heart-strings
filters the intoxication
that swells to ectasy.

Desire, dream and your visage, so bewitching!

तीन मन्ज़र

تین منظر

तसव्वुर

शोख़ियाँ मुज़तर निगाहे दीदए-सरशार में
इशरतें ख़्वाबीदा रंगे ग़ाज़ए रुख़सार में
सुर्ख़ होटों पर तबस्सुम की ज़ियाएं जिस तरह
यासमिन के फूल डूबे हों मये गुलनार में

تصوّر

شوخیاں مضطر نگاہِ دیدۂ سرشار میں
عشرتیں خوابیدہ رنگِ غازۂ رُخسار میں
سرخ ہونٹوں پر تبسم کی ضیائیں جس طرح
یاسمن کے پھول ڈوبے ہوں مئے گلنار میں

सामना

छनती हुई नज़रों से जज़बात की दुनियाँए
बे ख़्वाबियाँ, अफसाने, महताब, तमन्नायें
कुछ उलझी हुई बातें, कुछ बहके हुए नग़मे
कुछ अश्क जो आँखों से बेवज्ह छलक जाएं

سامنا

چھنتی ہوئی نظروں سے جذبات کی دنیائیں
بےخوابیاں، افسانے، مہتاب، تمنائیں
کچھ الجھی ہوئی باتیں، کچھ بہکے ہوئے نغمے
کچھ اشک جو آنکھوں سے بےوجہ چھلک جائیں

रुख़सत

फ़सुर्दा रुख़, लबों पर इक नयाज़ आमेज़ ख़ामोशी
तबस्सुम मुज़महिल था, मरमरीं हाथों में लरज़िश थी
वो कैसी बेकसी थी तेरी पुरतमकीं निगाहों में
वो क्या दुख था तेरी सहमी हुई ख़ामोश आहों में

رخصت

فسردہ رخ، لبوں پر اک نیاز آمیز خاموشی
تبسم مضمحل تھا، مرمریں ہاتھوں میں لرزش تھی
وہ کیسی بےکسی تھی تیری پُرتمکیں نگاہوں میں
وہ کیا دکھ تھا تری سہمی ہوئی خاموش آہوں میں

Three Scenes

Imagination

That playfulness, restless in her drunken eyes,
pleasures lurking in the talc's tints on her cheeks.
And on those crimson lips was her smile's glow
like jasmine dipped in the wine of flowers.

Encounter

A world of longing filtering through the eyes—
sleeplessness, tales, moon, yearnings.
Some tangled conversations, some stray strains—
and some tears in the eyes, for no reason.

Parting

Face woe-begone, on the lips silence tinged with humility,
the smile jaded and her marble hands aquiver.
What helplessness was there in your proud eyes
and what sorrow in your sighs, so mute and scared.

दोनों जहान तेरी मोहब्बत में हार के
वो जा रहा है कोई शबे ग़म गुज़ार के

دونوں جہان تیری محبت میں ہار کے
وہ جا رہا ہے کوئی شبِ غم گزار کے

वीरां है मैकदा, खुम-ओ-साग़र उदास हैं
तुम क्या गये के रुठ गये दिन बहार के

ویراں ہے میکدہ، خُم و ساغر اُداس ہیں
تم کیا گئے کہ روٹھ گئے دن بہار کے

इक फ़ुरसते-गुनाह मिली, वो भी चार दिन
देखे हैं हमने हौसले परवरदिगार के

اِک فرصتِ گناہ ملی، وہ بھی چار دن
دیکھے ہیں ہم نے حوصلے پروردگار کے

दुनियाँ ने तेरी याद से बेगाना कर दिया
तुम से भी दिलफ़रेब हैं गम रोज़गार के

دنیا نے تیری یاد سے بیگانہ کر دیا
تجھ سے بھی دلفریب ہیں غمِ روزگار کے

भूले से मुसकुरा तो दिए थे वो आज फ़ैज़
मत पूछ वलवले दिले नाकरदाकार के

بھُولے سے مسکرا تو دیئے تھے وہ آج فیضؔ
مت پوچھ ولولے دلِ ناکردہ کار کے

Losing Both Worlds . . .

Losing both worlds in his love for you,
there goes someone, after a night of pain.

Desolate is the tavern, and despondent are
the cups and jars—
your parting has alienated me from the days of spring.

Four days was all the time I had for sinning;
indeed, I've known the limits of God's bounty.

The world's grind has estranged me
from your remembrance—
the woes of life are more alluring than your love.

Unwittingly, as she broke into a smile today, O Faiz—
then ask me not how yearnings upsurged in this hapless
heart.

सोच

क्यूँ मेरा दिल शाद नहीं है
क्यूँ ख़ामोश रहा करता हूँ
छोड़ो मेरी राम कहानी
मैं जैसा भी हूँ अच्छा हूँ
मेरा दिल ग़मगीं है तो क्या
ग़मगीं ये दुनिया है सारी
ये दुख तेरा है न मेरा
हम सब की जागीर है प्यारी
तू गर मेरी भी हो जाये
दुनिया के ग़म यूँ ही रहेंगे
पाप के फंदे, जुल्म के बंधन
अपने कहे से कट न सकेंगे
ग़म हर हालत में मोहलिक है
अपना हो या और किसी का
रोना धोना, जी को जलाना
यूँ भी हमारा, यूँ भी हमारा
क्यूँ न जहाँ का ग़म अपना लें
बाद में सब तदबीरें सोचें
बाद में सुख के सपने देखें
सपनों की ताबीरें सोचें
बे-फ़िक्रे धन दौलत वाले
ये आख़िर क्यूँ खुश रहते हैं
इनका सुख आपस में बाँटें
ये भी आख़िर हम जैसे हैं
हम ने माना जंग कड़ी है
सर फूटेंगे, खून बहेगा
खून में ग़म भी बह जायेंगे
हम न रहें, ग़म भी न रहेगा

سوچ

کیوں میرا دل شاد نہیں ہے
کیوں خاموش رہا کرتا ہوں
چھوڑو میری رام کہانی
میں جیسا بھی ہوں اچھا ہوں
میرا دل غمگیں ہے تو کیا
غمگیں یہ دنیا ہے ساری
یہ دُکھ تیرا ہے نہ میرا
ہم سب کی جاگیر ہے پیاری
تو گر میری بھی ہو جائے
دنیا کے غم یوں ہی رہیں گے
پاپ کے پھندے، ظلم کے بندھن
اپنے کہے سے کٹ نہ سکیں گے
غم ہر حالت میں مہلک ہے
اپنا ہو یا اور کسی کا
رونا دھونا، جی کو جلانا
یوں بھی ہمارا، یوں بھی ہمارا
کیوں نہ جہاں کا غم اپنا لیں
بعد میں سب تدبیریں سوچیں
بعد میں سُکھ کے سپنے دیکھیں
سپنوں کی تعبیریں سوچیں
بے فکرے دھن دولت والے
یہ آخر کیوں خوش رہتے ہیں
ان کا سُکھ آپس میں بانٹیں
یہ بھی آخر ہم جیسے ہیں
ہم نے مانا جنگ کڑی ہے
سر پھوٹیں گے، خون بہے گا
خون میں غم بھی بہہ جائیں گے
ہم نہ رہیں، غم بھی نہ رہے گا

Reflections

Why is my heart so disconsolate?
Why am I always sunk in silence?
Leave me to my tale of woe
I'm happy as I am.

What if my heart is sorrowful,
Sorrow looms over the entire world.
This pain is neither yours nor mine,
it's every human's inheritance, O love.

Even if you were mine, O love,
the world's sorrows will remain—
embroilment in sin and tyranny's hold—
could we just wish them all away?

Sorrow is lethal in every form,
be it mine or somebody else's.
Tears only singe the heart—
this way or that, pain will always remain.

Why not own up the world's suffering
and later ponder over the way out?
There'll then be time for dreaming
and unravelling the riddle of dreams.

Carefree are all the affluent—
why are they always cheerful?
Let's share their joy and happiness,
for aren't they also like us?

Indeed, the struggle would be relentless,
heads will be bashed and blood will flow:
Blood will wash away all pain—
and as we perish so will end our suffering.

रात यूँ दिल में तेरी खोई हुई याद आयी
जैसे वीराने में चुपके से बहार आजाए
जैसे सहराओं में हौले से चले बादे नसीम
जैसे बीमार को बेवज्ह क़रार आ जाये

दिल रहीने ग़मे जहाँ है आज
हर नफ़्स तिशनाए फ़ुग़ाँ है आज
सख़्त वीराँ है महफ़िले हस्ती
ऐ ग़मे दोस्त तू कहाँ है आज

رات یوں دل میں تری کھوئی ہوئی یاد آئی
جیسے ویرانے میں چپکے سے بہار آ جائے
جیسے صحراؤں میں ہولے سے چلے بادِ نسیم
جیسے بیمار کو بے وجہ قرار آ جائے

دل رہینِ غمِ جہاں ہے آج
ہر نفس تشنہ فغاں ہے آج
سخت ویراں ہے محفلِ ہستی
اے غمِ دوست تو کہاں ہے آج

Quatrains

Last night, a fugitive memory of you slid into my heart
as though a wilderness was quietly touched by
springtide,
as though some breeze came soughing through a
desert,
or someone sick, for no reason, felt reclaimed.

Today my heart feels indebted to the sorrows of this
world.
Each breath is famished for lament.
How profoundly desolate is all concourse of life—
O pain of love, where are you today?

हसीनए ख़्याल से!

मुझे दे दे
रसीले होंट, मासूमाना पेशानी, हसीं आँखें
कि मैं इक बार फिर रंगीनियों में गर्क़ हो जाऊँ!
मेरी हस्ती को तेरी इक नज़र आग़ोश में ले ले
हमेशा के लिए उस दाम में महफ़ूज़ हो जाऊँ
ज़ियाए हुस्न से ज़ुलमाते दुनिया में न फिर आऊँ
गुज़िश्ता हसरतों के दाग़ मेरे दिल से धुल जाएँ
मैं आने वाले ग़म की फ़िक्र से आज़ाद हो जाऊँ
मेरे माज़ी व मुस्तक़बिल सरासर महव हो जाएँ
मुझे वो इक नज़र, इक जाविदानी सी नज़र दे दे

حسینۂ خیال سے!

مجھے دے دے
رسیلے ہونٹ، معصومانہ پیشانی، حسیں آنکھیں
کہ میں اک بار پھر رنگینیوں میں غرق ہو جاؤں
مری ہستی کو تیری اک نظر آغوش میں لے لے
ہمیشہ کے لئے اس دام میں محفوظ ہو جاؤں
ضیاءِ حسن سے ظلماتِ دنیا میں نہ پھر آؤں
گذشتہ حسرتوں کے داغ میرے دل سے دھل
جائیں
میں آنے والے غم کی فکر سے آزاد ہو جاؤں
مرے ماضی و مستقبل سراسر محو ہو جائیں
مجھے وہ اک نظر، اک جاودانی سی نظر دے دے

To My Love

Let me savour
those sweet lips, that innocent forehead
those beautiful eyes
that I may once again drown myself in fantasy.

Let a glance of yours gather up
my being into your lap
so I may rest, secure in this trap
never to return to life's darkness;
all stains of my past yearnings may be
washed off,
ridding me of the sable forebodings of the
future,
sweeping away all my yesterdays and
tomorrows
into oblivion.

Give me, my love, that one eternal glance—
just once!

वक़्फ़े हरमानो यास रहता है
दिल है, अक्सर उदास रहता है
तुम तो ग़म देके भूल जाते हो
मुझको एहसाँ का पास रहता है

وقفِ حرمان و یاس رہتا ہے
دل ہے، اکثر اداس رہتا ہے
تم تو غم دے کے بھول جاتے ہو
مجھ کو احساں کا پاس رہتا ہے

फ़ज़ाये दिल पे उदासी बिखरती जाती है
फ़सुर्दगी है के जाँ तक उतरती जाती है
फ़रेबे ज़ीस्त से कुदरत का मुद्आ मालूम
ये होश है के जवानी गुज़रती जाती है

فضائے دل پہ اُداسی بکھرتی جاتی ہے
فسردگی ہے کہ جاں تک اُترتی جاتی ہے
فریبِ زیست سے قدرت کا مدعا معلوم
یہ ہوش ہے کہ جوانی گزرتی جاتی ہے

Given Away to Sorrow and Despair

Given away to sorrow and despair,
my heart often wilts away.
Your offering of pain, you forget
while I cherish what you have gifted me.

In the ambience of my heart, sorrow sprawls,
despair seeps into my soul.
Life's illusion unfolds nature's intent—
all I'm conscious of is youth slipping away.

आज की रात

आज की रात साज़े-दर्द न छेड़
दुख से भरपूर दिन तमाम हुए
और कल की ख़बर किसे मालूम?
दोशो फ़र्दा की मिट चुकी हैं हुदूद
हो न हो अब सहर, किसे मालूम?
ज़िदंगी हेच! लेकिन आज की रात
एज़ दियत है मुमकिन आज की रात
आज की रात साज़े दर्द न छेड़
अब न दोहरा फसाना हाए अलम
अपनी क़िसमत पे सौ गवार न हो
फ़िक्रे फ़र्दा उतार दे दिल से
उम्रे रफ़्ता पे अश्क बार न हो
अहदे ग़म की हिकायतें मत पूछ
हो चुकीं सब शिकायतें मत पूछ
आज की रात साज़े-दर्द न छेड़

آج کی رات

آج کی رات سازِ درد نہ چھیڑ
دکھ سے بھرپور دن تمام ہوئے
اور کل کی خبر کسے معلوم؟
دوش و فردا کی مٹ چکی ہیں حدود
ہو نہ ہو اب سحر، کسے معلوم؟
زندگی ہیچ! لیکن آج کی رات
ایزدیت ہے ممکن آج کی رات
آج کی رات سازِ درد نہ چھیڑ
اب نہ دہرا فسانہ ہائے الم
اپنی قسمت پہ سوگوار نہ ہو
فکرِ فردا اُتار دے دل سے
عمرِ رفتہ پہ اشکبار نہ ہو
عہدِ غم کی حکایتیں مت پوچھ
ہو چکیں سب شکایتیں مت پوچھ
آج کی رات سازِ درد نہ چھیڑ

Tonight

Don't thrum those chords of sorrow tonight—
gone is all my anguished past,
and who knows what tomorrow holds out.

The bounds of past and future blurred,
who knows if dawn will ever break.

Futile this dreary existence—but no,
it's possible to be a god tonight.

Don't thrum those chords of sorrow tonight,
recall those tales of gloom
or lament over your fate.

Don't let dread of the future haunt your mind,
nor shed tears over days gone by.

Don't now ask how things went awry,
for I'm done with all complaining.
So no more those tales of sorrow—
not tonight.

एक मंज़र

बामो-दर ख़ामुशी के बोझ से चूर
आसमानों से जूए दर्द रवाँ
चाँद का दु:ख भरा फ़सानाए-नूर
शाहराहों की ख़ाक में ग़लताँ
ख़्वाबगाहों में नीम तारीकी
मुज़महिल लै रुबाबे हस्ती की
हल्के हल्के सुरों में नौहा कुनाँ

ایک منظر

بام و در خامشی کے بوجھ سے چور
آسمانوں سے جوئے درد رواں
چاند کا دکھ بھرا فسانۂ نور
شاہراہوں کی خاک میں غلطاں
خواب گاہوں میں نیم تاریکی
مضمحل لے ربابِ ہستی کی
ہلکے ہلکے سروں میں نوحہ کناں

A Scene

Terrace and door steeped in silence—
from the sky flows the river of desolation.
The moon's tragic tale of light
immersed in the dust of highways.
Semi-darkness in the chambers of night—and
the melody of life's lyre played out
in faint, elegiac strains.

मेरे नदीम

ख़्यालो-शेर की दुनिया में जान थी जिनसे
फ़ज़ाए फ़िक्रो अमल अरग़वान थी जिनसे
वो जिन के नूर से शादाब थे महो अंजुम
जुनूने इश्क़ की हिम्मत जवान थी जिनसे
वो आरज़ूएं कहाँ सो गयीं हैं मेरे नदीम?
वो नासुबूर निगाहें, वो मुन्तज़िर राहें
वो पासे ज़ब्त से दिल में दबी हुई आहें
वो इन्तेज़ार की रातें, तवील तीरओ-तार
वो नीम ख़्वाब शबिस्ताँ, वो मख़मलीं बाहें
कहानियाँ थीं, कहीं खो गयीं हैं, मेरे नदीम
मचल रहा है रगे ज़िन्दगी में ख़ूने बहार
उलझ रहे हैं पुराने ग़मों से रूह के तार
चलो के चल के चराग़ां करें दयारे हबीब
हैं इन्तेज़ार में अगली मोहब्बतों के मज़ार
मुहब्बतें जो फ़ना हो गयीं हैं मेरे नदीम!

میرے ندیم

خیال وشعر کی دنیا میں جان تھی جن سے
فضائے فکر وعمل ارغوان تھی جن سے
وہ جن کے نور سے شاداب تھے مہ وانجم
جنونِ عشق کی ہمت جوان تھی جن سے
وہ آرزوئیں کہاں سوگئی ہیں میرے ندیم؟
وہ ناصبور نگاہیں، وہ منتظر راہیں
وہ پاسِ ضبط سے دل میں دبی ہوئی آہیں
وہ انتظار کی راتیں، طویل تیرہ وتار
وہ نیم خواب شبستاں، وہ مخملیں باہیں
کہانیاں تھیں، کہیں کھوگئی ہیں، میرے ندیم
مچل رہا ہے رگ زندگی میں خون بہار
الجھ رہے ہیں پرانے غموں سے روح کے تار
چلو کہ چل کے چراغاں کریں دیارِ حبیب
ہیں انتظار میں اگلی محبتوں کے مزار
محبتیں جو فنا ہوگئی ہیں میرے ندیم!

My Friend

Those which were the soul of my fancy and verse,
lent their crimson to my thoughts, my deeds,
with whose effulgence glowed the moon and stars,
brought such courage to our love's frenzy—
where have those longings gone, my friend?

Those insatiate eyes, those waiting pathways,
those sighs in the heart for restraint
those nights of waiting, endless and dark—
those bedrooms, half-awake, those velvet arms—
mere yarns they were, where have they vanished,
my friend?

Sizzling in life's artery is spring's blood
the soul's strings entangled with past sorrows.
Let us go now and light up the house of the beloved
for lying in wait are the catacombs of past loves—
loves which have perished, my friend.

मुझ से पहली सी मोहब्बत मेरी महबूब न मांग

मुझसे पहली सी मोहब्बत मेरी महबूब न मांग
मैंने समझा था कि तू है तो दरख़्शां है हयात
तेरा ग़म है तो ग़मे-दहर का झगड़ा क्या है
तेरी सूरत से है आलम में बहारों को सबात
तेरी आँखों के सिवा दुनिया में रखा क्या है
तू जो मिल जाये तो तक़दीर निगूँ हो जाए
यू न था, मैं ने फ़क़त चाहा था यूँ हो जाए

और भी दुख हैं ज़माने में मोहब्बत के सिवा
राहतें और भी हैं वस्ल की राहत के सिवा

अनगिनत सदियों के तारीक़ बहीमाना तिलिस्म
रेशमो-अतलसो-कमख़्वाब में बुनवाये हुए
जाबजा बिकते हुए कूचा-ओ-बाज़ार में जिस्म
ख़ाक में लुथड़े हुए, ख़ून में नहलाये हुए
जिस्म निकले हुए इमराज़ के तन्नूरों से
पीप बहती हुई गलते हुए नासूरों से
लौट जाती है उधर को भी नज़र क्या कीजे
अब भी दिलकश है तेरा हुस्न मगर क्या कीजे
और भी दुख हैं ज़माने में मोहब्बत के सिवा
राहतें और भी हैं वस्ल की राहत के सिवा

मुझ से पहली सी मोहब्बत मेरी महबूब न मांग

مجھ سے پہلی سے محبت مری محبوب نہ مانگ

مجھ سے پہلی سی محبت مری محبوب نہ مانگ
میں نے سمجھا تھا کہ تو ہے تو درخشاں ہے حیات
تیرا غم ہے تو غمِ دہر کا جھگڑا کیا ہے
تیری صورت سے ہے عالم میں بہاروں کو ثبات
تیری آنکھوں کے سوا دنیا میں رکھا کیا ہے
تو جو مل جائے تو تقدیر نگوں ہو جائے
یوں نہ تھا، میں نے فقط چاہا تھا یوں ہو جائے

اور بھی دکھ ہیں زمانے میں محبت کے سوا
راحتیں اور بھی ہیں وصل کی راحت کے سوا

ان گنت صدیوں کے تاریک بہیمانہ طلسم
ریشم و اطلس و کمخواب میں بنوائے ہوئے
جا بجا بکتے ہوئے کوچہ و بازار میں جسم
خاک میں لتھڑے ہوئے خون میں نہلائے ہوئے
جسم سے نکلے ہوئے امراض کے تنوروں سے
پیپ بہتی ہوئی گلتے ہوئے ناسوروں سے
لوٹ جاتی ہے ادھر کو بھی نظر کیا کیجے
اب بھی دلکش ہے ترا حسن مگر کیا کیجے
اور بھی دکھ ہیں زمانے میں محبت کے سوا
راحتیں اور بھی ہیں وصل کی راحت کے سوا

مجھ سے پہلی سی محبت مری محبوب نہ مانگ

Ask Me Not for That Old Fervour

Ask me not for that old fervour, my love.
I had then imagined
that your love would spark off my being,
Counterpoise the giant agony of the world—
that your beauty would bring every spring to
eternal blossom.
And what else was there to cherish but
your eyes?
Once you were mine
would not fate itself bow to me?
I had only willed it all
but it was not to be,
for there are sorrows other than heartache,
joys other than love's rapture.
If there are spells of those dark, savage,
countless centuries—
bodies robed in silk, satin and velvet—
then aren't there also bodies
traded down streets and alleyways—
bodies smeared in dust, bathed in blood
bodies emerging from ovens of sickness
bodies with pus oozing from chronic sores?
If these images also seize my eye
even though your beauty still enthrals,
it's because there are sorrows other than
heartache,
joys other than love's rapture
So ask me not for that old fervour, my love.

रक़ीब से

आ कि वाबस्ता हैं उस हुस्न की यादें तुझ से
जिसने इस दिल को परीखाना बना रखा था
जिसकी उल्फ़त में भुला रखी थी दुनिया हमने
दहर को दहर का अफ़साना बना रखा था
आशना हैं तेरे क़दमों से वो राहें जिन पर
उसकी मदहोश जवानी ने इनायत की है
कारवाँ गुज़रे हैं जिनसे उसी रानाई के
जिसकी इन आँखों ने बेसूद इबादत की है
तुझसे खेली हैं वो महबूब हवाएँ जिनमें
उसके मलबूस की अफ़सुर्दा महक बाक़ी है
तुझ पे भी बर्सा है उस बाम से मेहताब का नूर
जिस में बीती हुई रातों की कसक बाक़ी है
तूने देखी है वो पेशानी, वो रुख़सार, वो होंट
ज़िन्दगी जिनके तसव्वुर में लुटा दी हमने
तुझ पे उठ्ठी हैं वो खोई हुई साहिर आँखें
तुझको मालूम है क्यों उम्र गँवा दी हमने
हम पे मुशतरका हैं एहसान ग़मे-उल्फ़त के
इतने एहसान कि गिनवाऊँ तो गिनवा न सकूँ
हमने इस इश्क़ में क्या खोया है क्या सीखा है
जुज़ तेरे और को समझाऊँ तो समझा न सकूँ

رقیب سے

آ کہ وابستہ ہیں اس حسن کی یادیں تجھ سے
جس نے اس دل کو پری خانہ بنا رکھا تھا
جس کی الفت میں بھلا رکھی تھی دنیا ہم نے
دہر کو دہر کا افسانہ بنا رکھا تھا
آشنا ہیں ترے قدموں سے وہ راہیں جن پر
اس کی مدہوش جوانی نے عنایت کی ہے
کارواں گزرے ہیں جن سے اسی رعنائی کے
جس کی ان آنکھوں نے بے سود عبادت کی ہے
تجھ سے کھیلی ہیں وہ محبوب ہوائیں جن میں
اس کے ملبوس کی افسردہ مہک باقی ہے
تجھ پہ بھی برسا ہے اُس بام سے مہتاب کا نور
جس میں بیتی ہوئی راتوں کی کسک باقی ہے
تو نے دیکھی ہے وہ پیشانی، وہ رخسار، وہ ہونٹ
زندگی جن کے تصور میں لٹا دی ہم نے
تجھ پہ اٹھی ہیں وہ کھوئی ہوئی ساحر آنکھیں
تجھ کو معلوم ہے کیوں عمر گنوا دی ہم نے
ہم پہ مشترکہ ہیں احسان غم الفت کے
اتنے احسان کہ گنواؤں تو گنوا نہ سکوں
ہم نے اس عشق میں کیا کھویا ہے کیا سیکھا ہے
جز ترے اور کو سمجھاؤں تو سمجھا نہ سکوں

To My Rival

O my rival, with you are associated my memories
of that face which made my heart a fairyland,
for whose love I'd forgotten this world,
letting its affairs sound like a yarn.

To your footfalls are known those pathways
along which her beauty has showered its gifts
along which have passed the caravans of her charm—
she, whom my eyes worshipped in vain.

With you have gambolled those love-laden winds
in which still lingers the sad fragrance of her dress.
On you has fallen, from her terrace,
that moonface's glow which still carries the pain of
past nights.

You have known that forehead, those cheeks, those lips
fantasizing which I've squandered away my life.
On you have risen those spellbinding eyes—
only you'd know why my life has been an endless
waste.

We have both shared the favours of love's sorrows—
far too many to count.
What we've learnt or lost in this affair,
I could explain to no one but you.

आजिज़ी सीखी, ग़रीबों की हिमायत सीखी
यासो-हिरमान के, दुख-दर्द के मानी सीखे
ज़ेरदस्तों के मसाएब को समझना सीखा
सर्द आहों के, रुख़े-ज़र्द के मानी सीखे
जब कहीं बैठ के रोते हैं वो बेकस जिनके
अश्क आँखों में बिलकते हुए सो जाते हैं
नातवानों के निवालों पे झपटते हैं उक़ाब
बाज़ू तोले हुए मँडलाते हुए आते हैं
जब कभी बिकता है बाज़ार में मज़दूर का गोश्त
शाहराहों पे ग़रीबों का लहू बहता है
आगसी सीने में रह-रह के उबलती है न पूछ
अपने दिल पर मुझे क़ाबू ही नहीं रहता है।

عاجزی سیکھی، غریبوں کی حمایت سیکھی
یاس وحرمان کے، دکھ درد کے معنی سیکھے
زیرِ دستوں کے مصائب کو سمجھنا سیکھا
سرد آہوں کے، رخِ زرد کے معنی سیکھے
جب کہیں بیٹھ کے روتے ہیں وہ بیکس جن کے
اشک آنکھوں میں بلکتے ہوئے سو جاتے ہیں
ناتوانوں کے نوالوں پہ جھپٹتے ہیں عقاب
بازو تولے ہوئے منڈلاتے ہوئے آتے ہیں
جب کبھی بکتا ہے بازار میں مزدور کا گوشت
شاہراہوں پہ غریبوں کا لہو بہتا ہے
آگ سی سینے میں رہ رہ کے ابلتی ہے نہ پوچھ
اپنے دل پر مجھے قابو ہی نہیں رہتا ہے

Humility I've learnt, sympathy for the poor,
learnt the meaning of despair, suffering and pain;
learnt to comprehend the miseries of the oppressed,
the meaning of cold sighs, of pallid faces.

Whenever those hapless creatures sit together to cry,
in whose eyes tears, bitterly shed, fall asleep,
and those destitute upon whose morsels swoop down
the vultures hovering above, poised on their wing—

whenever is traded in the market place the flesh of the labourer,
and on the highways flows the blood of the poor,
a sort of fire upsurges in my bosom
and I lose all hold over my heart.

तन्हाई

फिर कोई आया दिल-ए-ज़ार! नहीं कोई नहीं
राहरौ होगा, कहीं और चला जायेगा
ढल चुकी रात, बिखरने लगा तारों का ग़ुबार
लड़खड़ाने लगे ऐवानों में ख़्वाबीदा चिराग़
सो गई रस्ता तक-तक के हर इक राहगुज़ार
अजनबी ख़ाक ने धुँदला दिए क़दमों के सुराग़
गुल करो शम्एँ, बढ़ा दो मय-ओ-मीना-ओ-अयाग़
अपने बे-ख़्वाब किवाड़ों को मुक़फ़्फ़ल कर लो
अब यहाँ कोई नहीं, कोई नहीं आयेगा

تنہائی

پھر کوئی آیا دلِ زار! نہیں کوئی نہیں
راہرو ہوگا، کہیں اور چلا جائے گا
ڈھل چکی رات، بکھرنے لگا تاروں کا غبار
لڑکھڑانے لگے ایوانوں میں خوابیدہ چراغ
سو گئی راستہ تک تک کے ہر اک راہگزار
اجنبی خاک نے دھندلا دیئے قدموں کے سراغ
گل کرو شمعیں، بڑھا دو مے و مینا و ایاغ
اپنے بے خواب کواڑوں کو مقفّل کر لو
اب یہاں کوئی نہیں، کوئی نہیں آئے گا

Loneliness

Is someone out there again,
O my aggrieved heart?
No, perhaps some passer-by, bound elsewhere.

The night is snapping at the seams,
scattered is the cluster of stars
and down the hallways
the drowsy tapers are gasping away.

Tired of the long wait,
every highway has fallen asleep,
every footprint blurred by the alien dust.

Put out the lights,
Put away the cups and wine—
and those doors which kept vigil all night,
lock them all.

Nobody will come here now—
No one!

राज़े-उल्फ़त छुपा के देख लिया
दिल बहुत कुछ जला के देख लिया

راز الفت چھپا کے دیکھ لیا
دل بہت کچھ جلا کے دیکھ لیا

और क्या देखने को बाक़ी है
आप से दिल लगा के देख लिया

اور کیا دیکھنے کو باقی ہے
آپ سے دل لگا کے دیکھ لیا

वो मेरे हो के भी मेरे न हुए
उनको अपना बना के देख लिया

وہ مرے ہو کے بھی مرے نہ ہوئے
ان کو اپنا بنا کے دیکھ لیا

आज उनकी नज़र में कुछ हमने
सबकी नज़रें बचा के देख लिया

آج ان کی نظر میں کچھ ہم نے
سب کی نظریں بچا کے دیکھ لیا

फ़ैज़ तक्मील-ए-ग़म भी हो न सकी
इश्क़ को आज़मा के देख लिया

فیض تکمیل غم بھی ہو نہ سکی
عشق کو آزما کے دیکھ لیا

I've Tried Camouflaging My Love's Secret

I've tried camouflaging my love's secret—
but even afflicting my heart was of no avail.

What else is there for me to know
after losing my heart to you?

She's mine, and yet not quite;
I've tried making her my own.

Today I saw in her eyes something
unnoticed by anyone around.

O Faiz, I'd longed for sorrow's fruition,
but not even love could do it for me.

پھر حریفِ بہار ہو بیٹھے
جانے کس کس کو آج رو بیٹھے

تھی، مگر اتنی رائگاں بھی نہ تھی
آج کچھ زندگی سے کھو بیٹھے

تیرے در تک پہنچ کے لوٹ آئے
عشق کی آبرو ڈبو بیٹھے

ساری دنیا سے دور ہو جائے
جو ذرا تیرے پاس ہو بیٹھے

نہ گئی تیری بے رخی نہ گئی
ہم تری آرزو بھی کھو بیٹھے

فیض ہوتا رہے جو ہونا ہے
شعر لکھتے رہا کرو بیٹھے

फिर हरीफ़े-बहार हो बैठे
जाने किस-किस को आज रो बैठे

थी मगर इतनी रायगाँ भी न थी
आज कुछ ज़िन्दगी से खो बैठे

तेरे दर तक पहुँच के लौट आये
इश्क़ की आबरू डुबो बैठे

सारी दुनिया से दूर हो जाए
जो ज़रा तेरे पास हो बैठे

न गई तेरी बेरूख़ी न गई
हम तेरी आरज़ू भी खो बैठे

फ़ैज़ होता रहे जो होना है
शेर लिखते रहा करो बैठे

Again, I Am a Rival of Spring

Again, I am a rival of spring—
such is my sorrow today over friends lost.

Futile was life, but not so much—
today something seems to have faded out of my life.

Making it to your doorstep and then returning—
wasn't that tainting the fair name of love?

One moves away from the entire world
when one sits close beside you.

Never did you give up your indifference,
even though I've forsaken all yearning for you.

O Faiz, let things take their own course—
you'd better keep spinning out your verses.

चंद रोज़ और मेरी जान!

चंद रोज़ और मेरी जान! फ़क़त चंद ही रोज़
ज़ुल्म की छाँव में दम लेने पे मजबूर हैं हम
इक ज़रा और सितम सह लें, तड़प लें, रो लें
अपने अज्दाद की मीरास है माज़ूर हैं हम

जिस्म पर क़ैद है ज़ज़्बात पे ज़ंजीरें हैं
फ़िक्र महबूस है, गुफ़्तार पे ताज़ीरें हैं
अपनी हिम्मत है कि हम फिर भी जिये जाते हैं
ज़िन्दगी क्या किसी मुफ़लिस की क़बा है जिसमें
हर घड़ी दर्द के पैवंद लगे जाते हैं
लेकिन अब ज़ुल्म की मीयाद के दिन थोड़े हैं
इक ज़रा सब्र, कि फ़रियाद के दिन थोड़े हैं

अर्सा-ए-दहर की झुलसी हुई वीरानी में
हम को रहना है, पे यूं ही तो नहीं रहना है
अजनबी हाथों का बेनाम गराँ-बार सितम
आज सहना है, हमेशा तो नहीं सहना है
ये तेरे हुस्न से लिपटी हुई आलाम की गर्द
अपनी दो रोज़ा जवानी की शिकस्तों का शुमार
चाँदनी रातों का बेकार दहकता हुआ दर्द
दिल की बेसूद तड़प, जिस्म की मायूस पुकार
चंद रोज़ और मेरी जान! फ़क़त चंद ही रोज़

چندروز اور مری جان !

چند روز اور مری جان! فقط چند ہی روز
ظلم کی چھاؤں میں دم لینے پہ مجبور ہیں ہم
اور کچھ دیر ستم سہہ لیں، تڑپ لیں، رو لیں
اپنے اجداد کی میراث ہے معذور ہیں ہم

جسم پر قید ہے، جذبات پہ زنجیریں ہیں
فکر محبوس ہے، گفتار پہ تعزیریں ہیں
اپنی ہمت ہے کہ ہم پھر بھی جیے جاتے ہیں
زندگی کیا کسی مفلس کی قبا ہے جس میں
ہر گھڑی درد کے پیوند لگے جاتے ہیں
لیکن اب ظلم کی میعاد کے دن تھوڑے ہیں
اک ذرا صبر، کہ فریاد کے دن تھوڑے ہیں

عرصۂ دہر کی جھلسی ہوئی ویرانی میں
ہم کو رہنا ہے، پہ یونہی تو نہیں رہنا ہے
اجنبی ہاتھوں کا بے نام گرانبار ستم
آج سہنا ہے، ہمیشہ تو نہیں سہنا ہے
یہ ترے حسن سے لپٹی ہوئی آلام کی گرد
اپنی دو روزہ جوانی کی شکستوں کا شمار
چاندنی راتوں کا بے کار دہکتا ہوا درد
دل کی بے سود تڑپ، جسم کی مایوس پکار
چند روز اور مری جان! فقط چند ہی روز

A Few Days More, My Love

A few days more, my love, just a few days—
are we fated to live in tyranny's shadow.
Let us endure a little longer—
oppression, writhing and tears.

All this is our legacy; we are helpless.
Body imprisoned, emotions shackled,
thought chained and speech censored.
It's just our courage that keeps us going.
Life is a beggar's tunic that picks on
patches of pain each moment.
But now the days of tyranny are numbered.
Just a little patience,
since the days of entreaty are nearly done.

In this scorched wasteland of life,
we're destined to live, but not like this.
This nameless, heavy oppression of alien hands,
we may have to endure today, but not forever.
This dust of torments smearing your beauty—
this dwelling on frustrations of our passing youth,
this futile, throbbing pain of moonlit nights,
this vain writhing of the heart, the body's helpless cry—
a few days more, my love, just a few days!

कुत्ते

ये गलियों के आवारा बेकार कुत्ते
के बख़्शा गया जिन को ज़ौक़े गदाई
ज़माने की फटकार सरमाया उनका
जहाँ भर की धुतकार उनकी कमाई
न आराम शब को, न राहत सवेरे
गलाज़त में घर, नालियों में बसेरे
जो बिगड़ें तो एक दूसरे से लड़ा दो
ज़रा एक रोटी का टुकड़ा दिखा दो
ये हर एक की ठोकरें खाने वाले
ये फ़ाक़ों से उकता के मर जाने वाले

ये मज़लूम मख़लूक़ गर सर उठाए
तो इन्सान सब सरकशी भूल जाए
ये चाहें तो दुनिया को अपना बना लें
ये आक़ाओं की हड्डियाँ तक चबा लें
कोई इनको एहसासे ज़िल्लत दिलादे
कोई इनकी सोई हुई दुम हिला दे

کُتّے

یہ گلیوں کے آوارہ بے کار کُتّے
کہ بخشا گیا جن کو ذوقِ گدائی
زمانے کی پھٹکار سرمایہ ان کا
جہاں بھر کی دھتکار ان کی کمائی
نہ آرام شب کو، نہ راحت سویرے
غلاظت میں گھر، نالیوں میں بسیرے
جو بگڑیں تو اک دوسرے سے لڑا دو
ذرا ایک روٹی کا ٹکڑا دکھا دو
یہ ہر ایک کی ٹھوکریں کھانے والے
یہ فاقوں سے اُکتا کے مرجانے والے

یہ مظلوم مخلوق گر سر اٹھائے
تو انسان سب سرکشی بھول جائے
یہ چاہیں تو دنیا کو اپنا بنالیں
یہ آقاؤں کی ہڈیاں تک چبالیں
کوئی ان کو احساسِ ذلت دلا دے
کوئی ان کی سوئی ہوئی دُم ہلا دے

Dogs

Tramping about the streets aimlessly, these dogs,
born to the prerogative of beggary—
their only treasure is the world's scorn
their only wages, the world's reproof.

Not a moment's respite, day or night—
dirt their abode, drains their rest-houses.

If roused, they may be set one against the other,
just dangle before them a morsel of bread—
they who suffer everybody's kicks,
who'd tire and die of starvation.

If these destitutes were ever stirred up,
man would forget his imperiousness.
If only they willed, they'd reign supreme
for they could chew up even the bones of their
masters.

All this—
if only someone would awaken them to their ignominy,
shake their sagging tails
to action!

बोल

बोल, कि लब आज़ाद हैं तेरे
बोल, ज़ुबां अब तक तेरी है
तेरा सुतवाँ जिस्म है तेरा
बोल कि जां अब तक तेरी है
देख कि आहंगर की दुकाँ में
तुंद हैं शोले, सुर्ख़ हैं आहन
खुलने लगे क़ुफ़लों के दहाने
फैला हर ज़ंजीर का दामन
बोल, ये थोड़ा वक़्त बहुत है
जिस्मो-ज़ुबाँ की मौत से
बोल, कि सच ज़िंदा है अब तक
बोल, जो कुछ कहना है कह ले

بول

بول، کہ لب آزاد ہیں تیرے
بول، زباں اب تک تیری ہے
تیرا ستواں جسم ہے تیرا
بول کہ جاں اب تک تیری ہے
دیکھ کہ آہن گر کی دکاں میں
تند ہیں شعلے، سرخ ہیں آہن
کھلنے لگے قفلوں کے دہانے
پھیلا ہر اک زنجیر کا دامن
بول، یہ تھوڑا وقت بہت ہے
جسم و زباں کی موت سے پہلے
بول، کہ سچ زندہ ہے اب تک
بول، جو کچھ کہنا ہے کہہ لے

Speak Up!

Speak up, for your lips are not sealed
and your words are still your own.
This upright body is yours—
speak, while your soul is still your own.

Look there, in that smithy,
its red oven, fierce flames,
the padlocks are already opening their mouths
and each fetter is skirting around.

Speak up now, for time's running out.
Before your body and mind fade away,
tell us, for truth is not yet dead.

Speak
whatever you have to say!

मौजुए-सुख़न

गुल हई जाती है अफ़सुर्दा सुलगती हुई शाम
धुल के निकलेगी अभी चशमए-महताब से रात
और मुशताक़ निगाहों की सुनी जाएगी
और उन हाथों से मस होंगे ये तरसे हुए हात

उनका आँचल है, कि रुख़्सार, कि पैराहन है
कुछ तो है जिससे हुई जाती है चिलमन रंगीं
जाने उस ज़ुल्फ की मौहूम घनी छाओं में
टिमटिमाता है वो आवेज़ा अभी तक कि नहीं

आज फिर हुस्ने दिल आरा की वही धज होगी
वही ख़्वाबीदा सी आँखें, वही काजल की लकीर
रंगे रुख़्सार पे हलका सा वो ग़ाज़े का गुबार
संदली हाथ पे धुंधली सी हिना की तहरीर

अपने अफ़कार की, अशआर की दुनिया है यही
जाने मज़मूँ है यही, शाहिदे माना है यही

आज तक सुर्ख़ो-सिया सदियों के साये के तले
आदमो-हव्वा की औलाद पे क्या गुज़री है?
मौत और ज़ीस्त की रोज़ाना सफ़ आराई में
हम पे क्या गुज़रेगी, अजदाद पे क्या गुज़री है?

موضوعِ سخن

گل ہوئی جاتی ہے افسردہ سلگتی ہوئی شام
ڈھل کے نکلے گی ابھی چشمۂ مہتاب سے رات
اور مشتاق نگاہوں کی سنی جائے گی
اور ان ہاتھوں سے مس ہوں گے یہ ترسے ہوئے ہات

ان کا آنچل ہے، کہ رخسار، کہ پیراہن ہے
کچھ تو ہے جس سے ہوئی جاتی ہے چلمن رنگیں
جانے اس زلف کی موہوم گھنی چھاؤں میں
ٹمٹماتا ہے وہ آویزہ ابھی تک کہ نہیں

آج پھر حسن دل آرا کی وہی دھج ہوگی
وہی خوابیدہ سی آنکھیں، وہی کاجل کی لکیر
رنگ رخسار پہ ہلکا سا وہ غازے کا غبار
صندلی ہاتھ پہ دھندلی سی حنا کی تحریر

اپنے افکار کی، اشعار کی دنیا ہے یہی
جانِ مضموں ہے یہی، شاہدِ معنی ہے یہی

آج تک سرخ و سیہ صدیوں کے سائے کے تلے
آدم و حوا کی اولاد پہ کیا گزری ہے؟
موت اور زیست کی روزانہ صف آرائی میں
ہم پہ کیا گزرے گی، اجداد پہ کیا گزری ہے؟

Poesy's Domain

This evening, forlorn—its embers smouldering.
Out of the moon's spring will emerge night, cleansed—
and my eager eyes will be rewarded
as my impatient hands touch yours.

Is it her stole, her cheeks or her dress—
something surely lends the screen such colour.
I wonder if in the deep, faint shadow of your locks
there still glimmers that eardrop.

Today again, there'll be the same splendour
of that bewitching beauty,
the same drowsy eyes, the same streak of collyrium
on her cheek the mellowed tint of talc,
on her sandalwood palms a blurred line of henna.

This alone is the domain of my thoughts—
my verse, its sole quintessence.

Till today, in the shadow of centuries, sanguine
and sable,
what has been the lot of Adam's progeny?
In the daily battle-array of death and life,
how will it fare with us, how had it fared with
our ancestors?

उन दमकते हुए शहरों की फ़रावाँ मख़लूक़
क्यों फ़क़त मरने की हसरत में जिया करती है?
ये हसीं खेत, फटा पड़ता है जोबन जिनका
किस लिए इनमें फ़क़त भूख उगा करती है

ये हर एक सम्त पुरअसरार कड़ी दीवारें
जलबुझे जिनमें हज़ारों की जवानी के चराग़
ये हर एक गाम पे उन ख्वाबों की मक़तलगाहें
जिनके परतव से चराग़ाँ हैं हज़ारों के दिमाग़

ये भी हैं, ऐसे कई और भी मज़मूं होंगे
लेकिन उस शोख़ के आहिस्ता से खुलते हुए होंट
हाये उस जिस्म के कमबख़्त दिलआवेज़ खुतूत
आप ही कहिये कहीं ऐसे भी अफ़सूँ होंगे

अपना मौज़ुए सुख़न इनके सिवा और नहीं
तबए शायर का वतन इनके सिवा और नहीं

ان دمکتے ہوئے شہروں کی فراواں مخلوق
کیوں فقط مرنے کی حسرت میں جیا کرتی ہے؟
یہ حسیں کھیت، پھٹا پڑتا ہے جوبن جن کا!
کس لئے ان میں فقط بھوک اگا کرتی ہے

یہ ہر اک سمت پُراسرار کڑی دیواریں
جل بجھے جن میں ہزاروں کی جوانی کے چراغ
یہ ہر اک گام پہ اُن خوابوں کی مقتل گاہیں
جن کے پرتو سے چراغاں ہیں ہزاروں کے دماغ

یہ بھی ہیں، ایسے کئی اور بھی مضموں ہوں گے
لیکن اس شوخ کے آہستہ سے کھلتے ہوئے ہونٹ
ہائے اس جسم کے کمبخت دلآویز خطوط
آپ ہی کہئے کہیں ایسے بھی افسوں ہوں گے

اپنا موضوعِ سخن ان کے سوا اور نہیں
طبعِ شاعر کا وطن ان کے سوا اور نہیں

The jostling crowds of these glittering cities—
why do they sustain themselves on a mere death-wish?
These luscious corn-fields bursting with youth—
why do they yield hunger alone?

These impregnable, mysterious walls all around,
within which
were snuffed out the lamps of countless young
hearts.
At every step, these abattoirs of dreams
whose reflections have ignited the minds of multitudes.

All these themes are there indeed—and many more;
but the gently parting lips of that beauty—
and oh, the alluring contours of her body—
now tell me yourself, could there be such
witchery elsewhere?

Well, for me this is it—
a poet's mental province can be none other than this.

हम लोग

दिल के एवाँ में लिए गुलशुदा शमओं की क़तार
नूरे ख़ुरशीद से सहमे हुए उकताए हुए
हुस्ने महबूब के सय्याल तसव्वुर की तरह
अपनी तारीकी को भींचे हुए लिपटाए हुए

ग़ायते सूदो ज़ियाँ, सूरते आग़ाज़ो मआल
वही बेसूद तजस्सुस, वही बेकार सवाल
मुज़महिल साअते इमरोज़ की बेरंगी से
यादे माज़ी से ग़मीं, दहशते फ़रदा से निढ़ाल
तशना अफ़कार जो तसकीन नहीं पाते हैं
सोख़्ता अश्क जो आँखों में नहीं आते हैं
एक कड़ा दर्द कि जो गीत में ढ़लता ही नहीं
दिल के तारीक शिगाफ़ों से निकलता ही नहीं
और एक उलझी हुई मौहूम सी दरमाँ की तलाश
दश्तो-ज़िन्दा की हवस, चाके गिरेबाँ की तलाश

ہم لوگ

دل کے ایواں میں لئے گُل شدہ شمعوں کی قطار
نورِ خورشید سے سہمے ہوئے اکتائے ہوئے
حسن محبوب کے سیّال تصوّر کی طرح
اپنی تاریکی کو بھینچے ہوئے لپٹائے ہوئے

غایتِ سود وزیاں، صورتِ آغاز و مآل
وہی بے سود تجسس، وہی بے کار سوال
مضمحِل ساعتِ امروز کی بے رنگی سے
یادِ ماضی سے غمیں، دہشت فردا سے نڈھال
تشنہ افکار جو تسکین نہیں پاتے ہیں
سوختہ اشک جو آنکھوں میں نہیں آتے ہیں
اک کڑا درد کہ جو گیت میں ڈھلتا ہی نہیں
دل کے تاریک شگافوں سے نکلتا ہی نہیں
اور اک الجھی ہوئی موہوم سی درماں کی تلاش
دشت وزنداں کی ہوس، چاکِ گریباں کی تلاش

We People

Carrying in the hallways of our hearts
rows of extinguished lamps
bored and fearful of sunlight
like the mercurial image of the beloved's beauty,
hugging our darkness, wrapped up in it.

Our concern—loss and gain
beginning and end—
the same futile curiosity, the same pointless quest.
Fatigued by the greyness of the daily scene,
grieving over the remembrance of things past,
enervated by the dread of the future.

Unquenched thoughts, never satiated;
burnt-out tears that never well up in the eyes—
a harsh pain that never melts into a song,
never oozes from the heart's dark crevices.
And a quest, confused, ethereal, for some panacea,
a craving for the wilderness and the prison,
a quest for the ripped collar.

शाहराह

एक अफ़सुर्दा शाहराह है दराज़
दूर उफ़क़ पर नज़र जमाए हुए
सर्द मिट्‌टी पे अपने सीने के
सुरमगीं हुस्न को बिछाए हुए

जिस तरह कोई ग़मज़दा औरत
अपने वीराँकदे में महवे ख़याल
वसले महबूब के तसव्वुर में
मू ब मू चूर, अज़ू अज़ू निढ़ाल

شاہراہ

ایک افسردہ شاہراہ ہے دراز
دُور اُفق پر نظر جمائے ہوئے
سرد مٹی پہ اپنے سینے کے
سرمگیں حسن کو بچھائے ہوئے

جس طرح کوئی غمزدہ عورت
اپنے ویراں کدے میں محوِ خیال
وصلِ محبوب کے تصور میں
مو بہ مو چور، عضو عضو نڈھال

Highway

A sad highway, stretching endlessly—
its eyes riveted on the remote horizon.
The cold earth of its bosom
overspread with its grey beauty,

as though some woman grieving
in her desolate home,
immersed in thoughts
of union with her beloved—
each pore, each limb
limp with desire.

मताए लौहो क़लम छिन गयी तो क्या ग़म है
कि ख़ूने दिल में डूबो ली हैं उँगलियाँ मैंने
ज़ुबां पे मुहर लगी है तो क्या कि रख दी है
हर एक हलक़ए ज़ंजीर में ज़ुबां मैंने

तेरा जमाल निगाहों में लेके उठा हूँ
निखर गयी है फ़ज़ा तेरे पैरहन की सी
नसीम तेरे शबिस्ताँ से होके आयी हैं
मेरी सहर में महक है तेरे बदन की सी

متاعِ لوح وقلم چھن گئی تو کیا غم ہے
کہ خونِ دل میں ڈبو لی ہیں انگلیاں میں نے
زباں پہ مہر لگی ہے تو کیا کہ رکھ دی ہے
ہر ایک حلقۂ زنجیر میں زباں میں نے

ترا جمال نگاہوں میں لے کے اٹھا ہوں
نکھر گئی ہے فضا تیرے پیرہن کی سی
نسیم تیرے شبستاں سے ہو کے آئی ہے
مری سحر میں مہک ہے ترے بدن کی سی

Quatrains

What if my pen and paper have been snatched away,
I've dipped my fingers in the heart's blood,
What if my lips are sealed,
I've lent my tongue to each link in the chain.

Eyes drunk on your beauty, I rise—
the air feels spruced up like your robe.
The breeze must have wafted through your
bed-chamber,
so redolent of your body is my dawn.

ऐ दिले बेताब ठहर!

तीरगी है कि उमडती ही चली आती है
शब की रग रग से लहू फूट रहा हो जैसे
चल रही है कुछ इस अंदाज़ से नब्ज़े हस्ती
दोनों आलम का नशा टूट रहा हो जैसे
रात का गर्म लहू और भी बह जाने दो
यही तरीकी तो है ग़ाज़ाए रुख़्सारे सहर
सुब्ह होने ही को है ऐ दिले बेताब ठहर
अभी ज़ंजीर छनकती है पसे पर्दाए साज़
मुतलक़ुल हुक्म है शीराज़ाए असबाब अभी
साग़रे नाब में आँसू भी ढलक जाते हैं
लग़ज़िशे पा में है पाबंदीए आदाब अभी

अपने दीवानों को दीवाना तो बन लेने दो
अपने मयख़ानों को मयख़ाना तो बन लेने दो
जल्द ये सुतवते असबाब भी उठ जाएगी
ये गिरांबारीए आदाब भी उठ जाएगी
ख़्वाह ज़ंजीर छनकती ही, छनकती ही रहे

اے دلِ بیتاب ٹھہر!

تیرگی ہے کہ امڈتی ہی چلی آتی ہے
شب کی رگ رگ سے لہو پھوٹ رہا ہو جیسے
چل رہی ہے کچھ اس انداز سے نبضِ ہستی
دونوں عالم کا نشہ ٹوٹ رہا ہو جیسے
رات کا گرم لہو اور بھی بہہ جانے دو
یہی تاریکی تو ہے غازۂ رخسارِ سحر
صبح ہونے ہی کو ہے اے دل بیتاب ٹھہر
ابھی زنجیر چھنکتی ہے پس پردۂ ساز
مطلق الحکم ہے شیرازۂ اسباب ابھی
ساغرِ ناب میں آنسو بھی ڈھلک جاتے ہیں
لغزشِ پا میں ہے پابندیٔ آداب ابھی

اپنے دیوانوں کو دیوانہ تو بن لینے دو
اپنے میخانوں کو میخانہ تو بن لینے دو
جلد یہ سطوتِ اسباب بھی اٹھ جائے گی
یہ گرانبارئ آداب بھی اٹھ جائے گی
خواہ زنجیر چھنکتی ہی، چھنکتی ہی رہے

Hold On, Restless Heart

Darkness that's billowing up—
as though from every vein of the night, blood
gushes forth.
The pulse of life throbs
as the intoxication of both worlds fades away.

Hot blood of the night,
let it gush forth still more—after all,
this very darkness powders the dawn's cheeks.
It will soon be day—hold on, restless heart.

The chains still clank behind the screen of music,
the package of goods and chattel still holds its
inexorable sway.
In the red wine, even the tears get intermingled;
there's still
in the staggering feet the gesture of tamed greeting.

Let the frenzy of your lovers swell ever so high—
let your taverns for once be real.
Soon will the supremacy of goods and chattel be over
as also the heavy burden of cares,
even if the chains keep on clanking forever.

मेरे हमदम, मेरे दोस्त!

गर मुझे इसका यक़ीं हो मेरे हमदम, मेरे दोस्त!
गर मुझे इसका यक़ीं हो कि तेरे दिल की थकन
तेरी आँखों की उदासी, तेरे सीने की जलन
मेरी दिलजोई, मेरे प्यार से मिट जाएगी
गर मेरा हर्फ़े तसल्ली वो दवा हो जिस से
जी उठे फिर तेरा उजड़ा हुआ बेनूर दिमाग़
तेरी पेशानी से धुल जाएँ ये तज़लील के दाग़
तेरी बीमार जवानी को शिफ़ा हो जाए
गर मुझे इसका यक़ीं हो मेरे हमदम, मेरे दोस्त!
रोज़ो शब, शामो-सहर मैं तुझे बहलाता रहूँ
मैं तुझे गीत सुनाता रहूँ हल्के, शीरीं
आबशारों के, बहारों के, चमन ज़ारों के गीत
आमदे सुबह के, महताब के, सय्यारों के गीत

तुझ से मैं हुस्नो-मुहब्बत की हिकायात कहूँ
कैसे मग़रूर हसीनाओं के बरफ़ाब से जिस्म
गर्म हाथों की हरारत में पिघल जाते हैं
कैसे इक चेहरे के ठहरे हुए मानूस नक़ूश
देखते-देखते यक लख़्त बदल जाते हैं
किस तरह आरिज़े महबूब का शिफ़ाफ़ बिल्लौर
यकबयक बादाए अहमर से दहक जाता है
कैसे गुलचीं के लिए झुकती है खुद शाख़े गुलाब
किस तरह रात का ऐवान महक जाता है

مرے ہمدم، مرے دوست!

گر مجھے اس کا یقیں ہو مرے ہمدم، مرے دوست!
گر مجھے اس کا یقیں ہو کہ ترے دل کی تھکن
تیری آنکھوں کی اداسی، ترے سینے کی جلن
میری دلجوئی، مرے پیار سے مٹ جائے گی
گر مرا حرف تسلی وہ دوا ہو جس سے
جی اٹھے پھر ترا اجڑا ہوا بے نور دماغ
تیری پیشانی سے دھل جائیں یہ تذلیل کے داغ
تیری بیمار جوانی کو شفا ہو جائے
گر مجھے اس کا یقیں ہو مرے ہمدم، مرے دوست!
روز و شب، شام و سحر میں تجھے بہلاتا رہوں
میں تجھے گیت سناتا رہوں ہلکے، شیریں
آبشاروں کے، بہاروں کے، چمن زاروں کے گیت
آمدِ صبح کے، مہتاب کے، سیاروں کے گیت

تجھ سے میں حسن و محبت کی حکایات کہوں
کیسے مغرور حسیناؤں کے برفاب سے جسم
گرم ہاتھوں کی حرارت میں پگھل جاتے ہیں
کیسے اک چہرے کے ٹھہرے ہوئے مانوس نقوش
دیکھتے دیکھتے یک لخت بدل جاتے ہیں
کس طرح عارضِ محبوب کا شفاف بلور
یک بیک بادۂ احمر سے دہک جاتا ہے
کیسے گلچیں کے لئے جھکتی ہے خود شاخِ گلاب
کس طرح رات کا ایوان مہک جاتا ہے

My Friend, My Mate

If only I could be certain, my friend,
if only I could be sure that your heart's fatigue,
your eyes' despondency, your heartburn
will be healed by my consoling and my love,
        if my word of cheer were the cure
        to enliven your dull and desolate mind,
        wash off the stains of humiliation
        and heal your sick youth.
If only I could be certain, my friend,
I'd console you day and night, evening and morning,
humming to you songs, tender and sweet—
songs of waterfalls, of springs, of gardens,
of dawn's arrow, of the moon and the planets.
I'd tell you tales of beauty and love—of
the snow-cold bodies of proud and beautiful women
who melt in the heat of a passionate embrace—
how the still, familiar lines of a face
will change suddenly, unnoticed;
how the crystal of the beloved's cheeks
takes on the glow of red wine;
how the rose-stem offers itself to the
                    flower-gatherer,
and how the hallway of night
is filled with fragrance.

यूँ ही गाता रहूँ, गाता रहूँ तेरी ख़ातिर
गीत बुनता रहूँ, बैठा रहूँ तेरी ख़ातिर
पर मेरे गीत तेरे दुख का मुदावा ही नहीं
नग़मा जर्राह नहीं, मुनिसो ग़मख़्वार सही
गीत नश्तर तो नहीं, मरहमे आज़ार सही
तेरे आज़ार का चारा नहीं, नश्तर के सिवा
और ये सफ़्फ़ाक मसीहा मेरे क़ब्ज़े में नहीं
हाँ मगर तेरे सिवा, तेरे सिवा, तेरे सिवा

یونہی گاتا رہوں، گاتا رہوں تیری خاطر
گیت بنتا رہوں، بیٹھا رہوں تیری خاطر
پر مرے گیت تیرے دکھ کا مداوا ہی نہیں
نغمہ، جرّاح نہیں، مونس و غم خوار سہی
گیت نشتر تو نہیں، مرہمِ آزار سہی
تیرے آزار کا چارہ نہیں، نشتر کے سوا
اور یہ سفّاک مسیحا مرے قبضے میں نہیں
اس جہاں کے کسی ذی روح کے قبضے میں نہیں
ہاں مگر تیرے سوا، تیرے سوا، تیرے سوا

So would I keep on singing, sitting beside you,
weaving songs,
all for your sake.

But my songs are no cure for your pain—
a song is no surgeon even though it may be a
consoler;
music is no surgeon's knife even if it soothes
as a balm.
Your ailment has no cure save the lancet,
and this cruel cure is beyond me—
beyond anything that breathes on earth.
Yes, it rests with you,
only you!

सुबहे आज़ादी
अगस्त 47 ई.

ये दाग़ दाग़ उजाला, ये शबगज़ीदा सहर
वो इन्तज़ार था जिस का, ये वो सहर तो नहीं
ये वो सहर तो नहीं जिस की आरज़ू लेकर
चले थे यार कि मिल जाएगी कहीं न कहीं
फ़लक के दश्त में तारों की आख़री मंज़िल
कहीं तो होगा शबे-सुस्त मौज् का साहिल
कहीं तो जा के रुकेगा सफ़ीना-ए-ग़म-ए-दिल
जवाँ लहू की पुर-असरार शाहराहों से
चले जो यार तो दामन पे कितने हाथ पड़े
दयार-ए-हुस्न की बे-सब्र ख़्वाब-गाहों से
पुकारती रहीं बाहें, बदन बुलाते रहे
बहुत अज़ीज़ थी लेकिन रुख़-ए-सहर की लगन
बहुत क़रीं था हसीनाने-नूर का दामन
सुबुक सुबुक थी तमन्ना, दबी दबी थी थकन

صبحِ آزادی
اگست ۴۷ء

یہ داغ داغ اُجالا، یہ شب گزیدہ سحر
وہ انتظار تھا جس کا، یہ وہ سحر تو نہیں
یہ وہ سحر تو نہیں جس کی آرزو لے کر
چلے تھے یار کہ مل جائے گی کہیں نہ کہیں
فلک کے دشت میں تاروں کی آخری منزل
کہیں تو ہوگا شبِ سست موج کا ساحل
کہیں تو جا کے رکے گا سفینۂ غمِ دل
جواں لہو کی پراسرار شاہراہوں سے
چلے جو یار تو دامن پہ کتنے ہاتھ پڑے
دیارِ حسن کی بے صبر خواب گاہوں سے
پکارتی رہیں باہیں، بدن بلاتے رہے
بہت عزیز تھی لیکن رخِ سحر کی لگن
بہت قریں تھا حسینانِ نور کا دامن
سبک سبک تھی تمنا، دبی دبی تھی تھکن

The Morning of Freedom

August 1947

This daybreak, pockmarked—
this morning, night-bitten.
Surely, this is not the morning we'd longed for,
in whose eager quest, all comrades
had set out, hoping that somewhere
in the wilderness of the sky
would emerge the ultimate destination of stars;
somewhere, the wave of the slow night will meet
the shore
and somewhere will anchor the boat of
heart's grief.

As we friends set out on those mysterious highways
of young blood, how many hands caught us by
the sleeve?

From the dreamlands of beauty's pleasure-houses
kept beckoning to us, impatiently, seductive arms;
bodies called out to us.
But we yearned only for the morning's face,
even though within easy reach was the hem of
radiant beauties.
Delicate was our longing, and faint our sense of
exhaustion.

सुना है हो भी चुका है फ़िराक़-ए-ज़ुल्मत-ए-नूर
सुना है हो भी चुका है विसाल-ए-मंज़िल-ओ-गाम
बदल चुका है बहुत अहल-ए-दर्द का दस्तूर
निशात-ए-वस्ल हलाल-ओ-अज़ाब-ए-हिज्र-ए-हराम

जिगर की आग, नज़र की उमंग, दिल की जलन
किसी पे चारा-ए-हिज्रां का कुद्द असर ही नहीं
कहाँ से आई निगार-ए-सबा, किधर को गई
अभी चिराग़-ए-सर-ए-रह को कुछ ख़बर ही नहीं

अभी गरानि-ए-शब में कमी नहीं आई
नेजात-ए-दीद-ओ-दिल की घड़ी नहीं आई
चले चलो कि वो मंज़िल अभी नहीं आई

سنا ہے ہو بھی چکا ہے فراقِ ظلمت و نور
سنا ہے ہو بھی چکا ہے وصالِ منزل و گام
بدل چکا ہے، بہت اہلِ درد کا دستور
نشاطِ وصل حلال و عذابِ ہجر حرام

جگر کی آگ، نظر کی امنگ، دل کی جلن
کسی پہ چارۂ ہجراں کا کچھ اثر ہی نہیں
کہاں سے آئی نگارِ صبا، کدھر کو گئی
ابھی چراغِ سرِ رہ کو کچھ خبر نہیں

ابھی گرانیٔ شب میں کمی نہیں آئی
نجاتِ دیدہ و دل کی گھڑی نہیں آئی
چلے چلو کہ وہ منزل ابھی نہیں آئی

We hear now that light and darkness have parted—
also, that there's now a union of quest and goal,
that the lot of the afflicted is now changed,
that the pleasure of union is granted
and banished is the torment of separation.

Fire in the bosom, longing in the eyes, and
heartburn—
nothing can soothe the anguish of separation.
Where did the sweet breeze come from, and where did
it vanish—
the street lamp has no news yet.
Even the night's heaviness is just the same;
the moment of salvation has not yet arrived
for the heart and the eye.

So let's press on, as the destination is still far away.

लौहो क़लम

हम परवरिशे लौहो क़लम करते रहेंगे
जो दिल पे गुज़रती है रक़म करते रहेंगे
असबाबे ग़मे इश्क़ बहम करते रहेंगे
वीरानीए दौरां पे करम करते रहेंगे
हाँ तलख़िए अय्याम अभी और बढ़ेगी
हाँ अहले सितम, मशक़े सितम करते रहेंगे
मन्ज़ूर ये तलख़ी, ये सितम हमको गवारा
दम है तो मुदावाए अलम करते रहेंगे
मयख़ाना सलामत है तो हम सुरख़िए मय से
तज़ईने दरो-बामे हरम करते रहेंगे
बाक़ी है लहू दिल में तो हर अश्क से पैदा
रंगे लबो-रुख़्सारे सनम करते रहेंगे
इक तर्ज़े तग़ाफ़ुल है सो वो उनको मुबारक
इक अर्ज़े तमन्ना है सो हम करते रहेंगे

لوح و قلم

ہم پرورشِ لوح و قلم کرتے رہیں گے
جو دل پہ گزرتی ہے رقم کرتے رہیں گے
اسبابِ غمِ عشق بہم کرتے رہیں گے
ویرانئ دوراں پہ کرم کرتے رہیں گے
ہاں تلخئ ایام ابھی اور بڑھے گی
ہاں اہلِ ستم، مشقِ ستم کرتے رہیں گے
منظور یہ تلخی، یہ ستم ہم کو گوارا
دم ہے تو مُداوائے الم کرتے رہیں گے
مہ خانہ سلامت ہے تو ہم سرخئ مے سے
تزئینِ در و بامِ حرم کرتے رہیں گے
باقی ہے لہو دل میں تو ہر اشک سے پیدا
رنگِ لب و رخسارِ صنم کرتے رہیں گے
اک طرزِ تغافل ہے سو وہ ان کو مبارک
اک عرضِ تمنا ہے سو ہم کرتے رہیں گے

Pen and Paper

Forever will I nurture pen and paper,
forever express in words whatever my heart undergoes,
forever proffer ingredients of the sorrows of love
and quicken into life the wasteland of time.

Yes, the bitterness of time will keep on spawning,
just as the tyrants will persist in their cruelty.

Cheerfully, I'll give into bitterness, this tyranny too
I'll endure—
so long as there's breath, I'll seek ever new cures
for torments.
If the tavern still remains, I shall embellish every door
and balcony of the *haram* with the redness of wine.

If the heart is not drained of all blood, I'll colour
every tear
with the redness of the beloved's lips and cheeks.

This posture of indifference, let it be her prerogative—
for me it will always be my desire's entreaty.

तुम आये हो न शब-ए-इन्तज़ार गुज़री है
तलाश में है सहर, बार-बार गुज़री है

जुनूँ में जितनी भी गुज़री बकार गुज़री है
अगर्चे दिल पे ख़राबी हज़ार गुज़री है

हुई है हज़रत-ए-नासेह से गुफ़्तगू जिस शब
वो शब ज़रूर सर-ए-कू-ए-यार गुज़री है

वो बात सारे फ़साने में जिसका ज़िक्र न था
वो बात उनको बहुत ना-गवार गुज़री है

न गुल खिले हैं, न उनसे मिले, न मैं पी है
अजीब रंग में अब के बहार गुज़री है

चमन में ग़ारत-ए-गुलचीं से जाने क्या गुज़री
क़फ़स से आज सबा बेक़रार गुज़री है

تم آے ہو، نہ شبِ انتظار گزری ہے
تلاش میں ہے سحر، بار بار گزری ہے

جنوں میں جتنی بھی گزری' بکار گزری ہے
اگر چہ دل پہ خرابی ہزار گزری ہے

ہوئی ہے حضرتِ ناصح سے گفتگو جس شب
وہ شب ضرور سرِ کوئے یار گزری ہے

وہ بات سارے فسانے میں جس کا ذکر نہ تھا
وہ بات ان کو بہت ناگوار گزری ہے

نہ گل کھلے ہیں، نہ ان سے ملے، نہ مے پی ہے
عجیب رنگ میں اب کے بہار گزری ہے

چمن پہ غارت گلچیں سے جانے کیا گزری
قفس سے آج صبا بے قرار گزری ہے

Neither Have You Come

Neither have you come, nor has ended the long
night of wait.
Even the breeze has whisked about, time and again,
seeking you.

Whatever time's spent in frenzy is well spent,
even if the heart has taken on a thousand
mishaps.

The night spent in confabulation with the adviser
was surely the one spent also down the beloved's lane.
what was never intended in the tale
is primarily that which has piqued her most.
No flowers blooming, no rendezvous, no wine—
how strangely has spring passed away this time.

Nobody knows what befell the garden, in
the wake
of the flower-gatherer's pillage—
so restlessly has the breeze flit past the
nest today.

तुम्हारी याद के जब ज़ख़्म भरने लगते हैं
किसी बहाने तुम्हें याद करने लगते हैं

हदीस-ए-यार के उनवाँ निखरने लगते हैं
तो हर हरीम में गेसू सँवरने लगते हैं

हर अजनबी हमें महरम दिखाई देता है
जो अब भी तेरी गली से गुज़रने लगते हैं

सबा से करते हैं गुर्बत-नसीब ज़िक्र-ए-वतन
तो चश्म-ए-सुबह में आँसू उभरने लगते हैं

वो जब भी करते हैं इस नुत्क़-ओ-लब की बख़ियागरी
फ़ज़ा में और भी नग़्में बिखरने लगते हैं

दर-ए-क़फ़स पे अँधेरे की मुहर लगती है
तो फ़ैज़ दिल में सितारे उतरने लगते हैं

تمہاری یاد کے جب زخم بھرنے لگتے ہیں
کسی بہانے تمہیں یاد کرنے لگتے ہیں

حدیثِ یار کے عنواں نکھرنے لگتے ہیں
تو ہر حریم میں گیسو سنورنے لگتے ہیں

ہر اجنبی ہمیں محرم دکھائی دیتا ہے
جو اب بھی تیری گلی سے گزرنے لگتے ہیں

صبا سے کرتے ہیں غربت نصیب ذکرِ وطن
تو چشمِ صبح میں آنسو اُبھرنے لگتے ہیں

وہ جب بھی کرتے ہیں اس نطق ولب کی بخیہ گری
فضا میں اور بھی نغمے بکھرنے لگتے ہیں

درِ قفس پہ اندھیرے کی مہر لگتی ہے
تو فیض دل میں ستارے اُترنے لگتے ہیں

When the Scars of Memory Begin to Heal

When the scars of memory begin to heal,
I think of you on one pretext or the other.
As the word of my beloved blossoms
every woman begins to groom her hair.
Every stranger appears to be a confidant,
even now when I pass through your lane.
Whenever the exiles talk to the breeze of their
homeland,
tears well up in the morning's eyes.
Whenever our lips are sewn up
still more the air resounds with songs.
As darkness seals the prison door,
stars illumine the heart, O Faiz.

शफ़क़ की राख में जल-बुझ गया सितारा-ए-शाम
शबे-फ़िराक़ के गेसू फ़ज़ा में लहराए
कोई पुकारो कि इक उम्र होने आयी है
फ़लक को क़ाफ़िला-ए-रोज़ो-शाम ठहराए
ये ज़िद है यादे-हरीफ़ाने-बादा पैमां की
कि शब को चांद न निकले, न दिन को अब्र आये
सबा ने फिर दरे-ज़िंदां पे आ के दी दस्तक
सहर क़रीब है, दिल से कहो न घबराये

شفق کی راکھ میں جل بجھ گیا ستارۂ شام
شبِ فراق کے گیسو فضا میں لہرائے
کوئی پکارو کہ اک عمر ہونے آئی ہے
فلک کو قافلۂ روز و شام ٹھہرائے
یہ ضد ہے یادِ حریفانِ بادہ پیما کی
کہ شب کو چاند نہ نکلے، نہ دن کو ابر آئے
صبا نے پھر درِ زنداں پہ آ کے دی دستک
سحر قریب ہے، دل سے کہو نہ گھبرائے

The Evening Star Has Burnt Out

The evening star has burnt out in dusk's ashes—
in the air wave the locks of the parting night.

Let someone proclaim life is running itself out,
the sky has held up the caravan of morning and
evening.

This is their obduracy, these enemies of wine
and cup—
let there be no moon by night, no cloud by day.

The breeze has knocked at the prison door again:
dawn is about to break, tell the heart not to feel
so restive.

दो इश्क़

(1)

ताज़ा हैं अभी याद में ऐ साक़ीए गुलफ़ाम
वो अक्स रुखे़ यार से महके हुए अय्याम
वो फूल सी खिलती हुई दीदार की साअत
वो दिल सा धड़कता हुआ उम्मीद का हंगाम
उम्मीद के लो जागा ग़मे दिल का नसीबा
लो शौक़ की तरसी हुई शब हो गयी आख़िर
लो डूब गये दर्द के बे ख़्वाब सितारे
अब चमकेगा बेसब्र निगाहों का मुक़द्दर
इस बाम से निकलेगा तेरे हुस्न का ख़ुरशीद
इस कुंज से फूटेगी किरण रंगे हिना की
इस दर से बहेगा तेरी रफ़्तार का सीमाब
उस राह पे फूलेगी शफ़क़ तेरी क़बा की
फिर देखे हैं वो हिज्र के तपते हुए दिन भी
जब फ़िक्र दिलो जाँ में फ़ुग़ाँ भूल गयी है
हर शब वो स्याह बोझ के दिल बैठ गया है
हर सुबह की लौ तीर-सी सीने में लगी है
तन्हाई में क्या क्या न तुझे याद किया है
क्या क्या न दिले ज़ार ने ढूंढी है पनाहें
आँखों से लगाया है कभी दस्ते सबा को
डाली है कभी गर्दने महताब में बाहें

دو عشق

(۱)

تازہ ہیں ابھی یاد میں اے ساقیِ گلفام
وہ عکسِ رُخِ یار سے لہکے ہوئے ایّام
وہ پھُول سی کھلتی ہوئی دیدار کی ساعت
وہ دل سا دھڑکتا ہُوا امّید کا ہنگام
امید کہ لو جاگا غمِ دل کا نصیبہ
لو شوق کی ترسی ہوئی شب ہو گئی آخر
لو ڈوب گئے درد کے بے خواب ستارے
اب چمکے گا بے صبر نگاہوں کا مقدّر
اس بام سے نکلے گا ترے حسن کا خورشید
اس کنج سے پھوٹے گی کرن رنگِ حنا کی
اِس در سے بہے گا تری رفتار کا سیماب
اُس راہ پہ پھولے گی شفق تیری قبا کی
پھر دیکھے ہیں وہ ہجر کے تپتے ہوئے دن بھی
جب فکرِ دل و جاں میں فغاں بھول گئی ہے
ہر شب وہ سیہ بوجھ کہ دل بیٹھ گیا
ہر صبح کی لو تیر سی سینے میں لگی ہے
تنہائی میں کیا کیا نہ تجھے یاد کیا ہے
کیا کیا نہ دلِ زار نے ڈھونڈی ہیں پناہیں
آنکھوں سے لگایا ہے کبھی دستِ صبا کو
ڈالی ہیں کبھی گردنِ مہتاب میں باہیں

Two Loves

I

Still green are the memories, O beautiful cup-bearer—
those days glowing with reflections from that face,
the moment of meeting, like a bud opening out,
that instant of hope, like a heart-throb.

Lo, the heartache is now recompensed,
ending at last the night's yearning.
Lo, the dreamless stars of pain are gone,
now the eager eyes' fortune will be rekindled.

From the terrace will emerge your beauty's sun,
from that niche shoot out the ray of henna's tint;
from this doorstep will flow your footstep's quicksilver,
and on that pathway glow your tunic's twilight.

Again have I also seen those scorching days of parting
when lament had forgotten itself, brooding over love
and life.

Each night so much burden wearing down my heart,
each morning's glow, piercing the heart like an arrow.

How often have I remembered you in my loneliness,
how many shelters has my aggrieved heart not sought?
Sometimes I have let the breeze's palm caress my eyes
and sometimes put my arms around the moon's nape.

(2)

चाहा है इसी रंग में लैलाए वतन को
तड़पा है इसी तौर से दिल उसकी लगन में
ढूंढी है यूँ ही शौक़ ने आसाइशे मंज़िल
रुख़सार के ख़म में कभी काकुल की शिकन में
उस जाने जहाँ को भी यूँ ही क़ल्बो नज़र ने
हंस हंस के सदा दी, कभी रो-रो के पुकारा
पूरे किये सब हर्फ़े तमन्ना के तक़ाज़े
हर दर्द को उजयाला, हर एक ग़म को संवारा
वापस नहीं फेरा कोई फ़रमान जुनूँ का
तन्हा नहीं लौटी कभी आवाज़ जरस की
ख़ैरियते जाँ, राहते तन, सेहते दामाँ
सब भूल गयीं मसलहते अहले हवस की
इस राह में जो सब पे गुज़रती है वो गुज़री
तन्हा पसे ज़िन्दाँ, कभी रुसवा सरे बाज़ार
गरजे हैं बहुत शेख़ सरेगोशए मिमबर
कड़के हैं बहुत अहले हकम बरसरे दरबार
छोड़ा नहीं ग़ैरों ने कोई नावके दुशनाम
छूटी नहीं अपनों से कोई तर्ज़े मलामत
इस इश्क़, न उस इश्क़ पे नादिम है मगर दिल
हर दाग़ है इस दिल में बजुज़ दाग़े नेदामत

(۲)

چاہا ہے اسی رنگ میں لیلائے وطن کو
تڑپا ہے اسی طور سے دل اس کی لگن میں
ڈھونڈی ہے یونہی شوق نے آسائشِ منزل
رخسار کے خم میں کبھی کاکل کی شکن میں
اس جانِ جہاں کو بھی یوں ہی قلب و نظر نے
ہنس ہنس کے صدا دی، کبھی رو رو کے پکارا
پورے کئے سب حرفِ تمنّا کے تقاضے
ہر درد کو اُجیالا، ہر اک غم کو سنوارا
واپس نہیں پھیرا کوئی فرمان جنوں کا
تنہا نہیں لوٹی کبھی آواز جرس کی
خیریتِ جاں، راحتِ تن، صحتِ داماں
سب بھول گئیں مصلحتیں اہلِ ہوس کی
اِس راہ میں جو سب پہ گزرتی ہے وہ گزری
تنہا پسِ زنداں، کبھی رسوا سرِ بازار
گرجے ہیں بہت شیخ سرِ گوشۂ منبر
کڑکے ہیں بہت اہلِ حکم برسرِ دربار
چھوڑا نہیں غیروں نے کوئی ناوکِ دشنام
چھوٹی نہیں اپنوں سے کوئی طرزِ ملامت
اس عشق، نہ اُس عشق پہ نادم ہے مگر دل
ہر داغ ہے اس دل میں بجز داغِ ندامت

II

Just so, have I craved for my Laila, my land,
my heart fluttered with the same longing;
just so has passion sought fulfilment—
sometimes in the cheek's curve, at times in the
lock's curl.
And so have the heart and the eye called out to
the other beloved,
sometimes through laughter, at times through tears—
and fulfilled all demands of desire;
kindled every pain and cared for every sorrow.
Never turned down any of frenzy's commands,
never renounced all worldly compromises—
life's security, body's comfort, hem's safety.

Much has the priest roared from the pulpit,
and much has the ruler thundered in the open court.
Never did my enemies share the barb of abuse
nor did my friends forsake their style of censure.

I have no regrets over this love or that—
my heart carries all the stains—
except remorse.

निसार में तेरी गलियों के...

निसार में तेरी गलियों के ए वतन कि जहाँ
चली है रस्म कि कोई न सर उठा के चले
जो कोई चाहने वाला तवाफ़ को निकले
नज़र चुरा के चले, जिस्म-ओ-जाँ बचा के चले
है अहल-ए-दिल के लिए अब ये नज़्म-ए-बस्त-ओ-कुशाद
कि संग-ओ-ख़िश्त मुक़य्द हैं और सग आज़ाद
बहुत है जुलम के दस्त-ए-बहाना-जू के लिए
जो चंद अहल-ए-जुनूँ तेरे नाम लेवा है
बने हैं अहल-ए-हवस मुद्दई भी, मुंसिफ़ भी
किसे वकील करें, किस से मुंसिफ़ी चाहें
मगर गुज़ारने वालों के दिन गुज़रते हैं
तेरे फ़िराक़ में यूँ सुबह-ओ-शाम करते हैं

बुझा जो रौज़न-ए-ज़िंदाँ तो दिल ये समझा है
कि तेरी मांग सितारों से भर गई होगी
चमक उठे हैं सलासिल तो हमने जाना है
कि अब सहर तेरे रुख़ पर बिखर गई होगी

نثار میں تیری گلیوں کے...

نثار میں تری گلیوں کے اے وطن کہ جہاں
چلی ہے رسم کہ کوئی نہ سر اُٹھا کے چلے
جو کوئی چاہنے والا طواف کو نکلے
نظر چُرا کے چلے، جسم وجاں بچا کے چلے
ہے اہل دل کے لئے اب یہ نظمِ بست وکشاد
کہ سنگ وخشت مقید ہیں اور سگ آزاد
بہت ہے ظلم کے دستِ بہانہ جو کے لئے
جو چند اہل جنوں تیرے نام لیوا ہیں
بنے ہیں اہل ہوس، مدّعی بھی، منصف بھی
کسے وکیل کریں، کس سے منصفی چاہیں
مگر گزارنے والوں کے دن گزرتے ہیں
ترے فراق میں یوں صبح وشام کرتے ہیں

بجھا جو روزنِ زنداں تو دل یہ سمجھا ہے
کہ تیری مانگ ستاروں سے بھر گئی ہوگی
چمک اُٹھے ہیں سلاسل تو ہم نے جانا ہے
کہ اب سحر ترے رُخ پر بکھر گئی ہوگی

Dedicated to Your Alleyways

I'm dedicated to your alleyways, O my motherland,
where it's customary now that nobody may walk
about, head held high.
If anyone dare step out, he must do so in furtive fear
of body and soul.
All your devotees must now withstand a new law,
a new order—
'Stones and bricks enchained, but dogs out at large.'

There's enough to provoke tyranny's hand, seeking
pretexts—
those few ardent devotees who still cherish your name.
These power-mongers are now both judges and
petitioners—
who then will defend us, and where shall we seek
justice?

But there are some who must perforce spend their days
banished from you, this is how their mornings and
evenings grind on.

As the cell's slit grows dim
my heart imagines your hair studded with stars,
and as the fetters become visible,
dawn, I imagine, must have lit up your face.

ग़रज़ तसव्वुर-ए-शाम-ओ सहर में जीते हैं
गिरफ़्त-ए-साया-ए-दीवार-ओ-दर में जीते हैं
यूँ ही हमेशा उलझती रही है ज़ुल्म से ख़ल्क़
न उनकी रस्म नई है, न अपनी रीत नई
यूँ ही हमेशा खिलाये हैं हमने आग में फूल
न उनकी हार नई है न अपनी जीत नई
इसी सबब से फ़लक का गिला नहीं करते
तेरे फ़िराक़ में हम दिल बुरा नहीं करते

गर आज तुझसे जुदा हैं तो कल बहम होंगे
ये रात भर की जुदाई तो कोई बात नहीं
गर आज औज पे है ताल-ए-रक़ीब तो क्या
ये चार दिन की ख़ुदाई तो कोई बात नहीं
जो तुझसे अहद-ए-वफ़ा उस्तवार रखते हैं
इलाज-ए-गर्दिश-ए-लैल-ओ-नहार रखते हैं

غرض تصوّرِ شام وسحر میں جیتے ہیں
گرفتِ سایۂ دیوار ودر میں جیتے ہیں
یوں ہی ہمیشہ الجھتی رہی ہے ظلم سے خلق
نہ ان کی رسم نئی ہے، نہ اپنی ریت نئی
یوں ہی ہمیشہ کھلائے ہیں ہم نے آگ میں پھول
نہ ان کی ہار نئی ہے نہ اپنی جیت نئی
اِسی سبب سے فلک کا گلہ نہیں کرتے
ترے فراق میں ہم دل بُرا نہیں کرتے

گر آج تجھ سے جُدا ہیں تو کل بہم ہوں گے
یہ رات بھر کی جدائی تو کوئی بات نہیں
گر آج اوَج پہ ہے طالعِ رقیب تو کیا
یہ چار دن کی خدائی تو کوئی بات نہیں
جو تجھ سے عہدِ وفا استوار رکھتے ہیں
علاجِ گردشِ لیل ونہار رکھتے ہیں

So I live on these fantasies, held by the shadows
of doors and walls, mornings and evenings.

The same age-old war between tyrants and mankind—
never have their ways changed, nor ours.
Always, we have let flowers bloom in fire.
It's always been the same—their defeat, our triumph.
That's why we've no grievance against our destiny,
no gloom over our separation from you.

If today we part, tomorrow's for reunion—
this brief spell of a night's separation is no matter.
If the rival's star towers high today,
this transient supremacy is of no consequence.
Only those committed to you deeply
hold the answer to the whirligig of time.

दिल में अब यूँ तेरे भूले हुये ग़म आते हैं
जैसे बिछड़े हुये काबे में सनम आते हैं
एक इक कर के हुये जाते हैं तारे रौशन
मेरी मंज़िल की तरफ़ तेरे क़दम आते हैं
रक़्से-मय तेज़ करो, साज़ की लय तेज करो
सू-ए-मैख़ाना सफ़ीराने-हरम आते हैं
कुछ हमीं को नहीं एहसान उठाने का दिमाग़
वो तो जब आते हैं माएल-ब-करम आते हैं
और कुछ देर न गुज़रे शब-ए-फ़ुर्क़त से कहो
दिल भी कम दुखता है, वो याद भी कम आते हैं

دل میں اب یوں ترے بھُولے ہوئے غم آتے ہیں
جیسے بچھڑے ہوئے کعبے میں صنم آتے ہیں
ایک اک کر کے ہوئے جاتے ہیں تارے روشن
میری منزل کی طرف تیرے قدم آتے ہیں
رقصِ مے تیز کرو، ساز کی لے تیز کرو
سوئے مے خانہ سفیرانِ حرم آتے ہیں
کچھ ہمیں کو نہیں احسان اٹھانے کا دماغ
وہ تو جب آتے ہیں، مائل بہ کرم آتے ہیں
اور کچھ دیر نہ گزرے شبِ فرقت سے کہو
دل بھی کم دُکھتا ہے' وہ یاد بھی کم آتے ہیں

In My Heart Now Well Up

In my heart now well up your long-forgotten sorrows
as though some forsaken idol returns to the *kaaba*.

One by one the stars are coming alive—
your footfalls are drawing close to my destination.

Pep up the tempo of the wine-dance, let the music
swell to its crescendo—
to the tavern come the emissaries of the *haram*.

It is I alone who would not seek favours,
although she is even willing to oblige.

Tell the night of separation to hold itself awhile,
for the heart now aches less and remembrance too
is faint.

अब वही हर्फ़-ए-जुनूँ सब की ज़ुबाँ ठहरी है
जो भी चल निकली है वो बात कहाँ ठहरी है

आज तक शैख़ के इकराम में जो शय थी हराम
अब वही दुशमने दीं, राहते जाँ ठहरी है

है ख़बर गर्म कि फिरता है गुरेज़ाँ नासेह
गुफ़्तगू आज सर-ए-कू-ए-बुताँ ठहरी है

है वही आरिज़-ए-लैला, वही शीरीँ का दहन
निगह-ए-शौक़ घड़ी भर को जहाँ ठहरी है

वस्ल की शब थी तो किस दर्जा सुबुक गुज़री थी
हिर्ज की शब है तो क्या सख़्त गरां ठहरी है

बिखरी एक बार तो हाथ आई है कब मौज-ए-शमीम
दिल से निकली है तो कब लब पे फ़ुग़ाँ ठहरी है

اب وہی حرفِ جنوں سب کی زباں ٹھہری ہے
جو بھی چل نکلی ہے وہ بات کہاں ٹھہری ہے

آج تک شیخ کے اکرام میں جو شے تھی حرام
اب وہی دشمنِ دیں، راحتِ جاں ٹھہری ہے

ہے خبر گرم کہ پھرتا ہے گریزاں ناصح
گفتگو آج سرِ کوئے بتاں ٹھہری ہے

ہے وہی عارضِ لیلیٰ وہی شیریں کا دہن
نگہِ شوق گھڑی بھر کو جہاں ٹھہری ہے

وصل کی شب تھی تو کس درجہ سُبک گزری تھی
ہجر کی شب ہے تو کیا سخت گراں ٹھہری ہے
بکھری اک بار تو ہاتھ آئی ہے کب موجِ شمیم
دل سے نکلی ہے تو کب لب پہ فغاں ٹھہری ہے

It's the Same Word of Passion

It's the same word of passion on everybody's lips;
how can a word be muzzled once it gets moving
around?

Till today, whatever was held taboo in the priest's
esteem,
the same has now become the unbeliever's credo, the
soul's repose.

It's strongly rumoured that the adviser is dodging
everyone,
for today he's engaged to hold a talk down the
beloved's lane.

There's the same Laila's cheek, the same mouth of
Shirin,
on whomsoever has the fond eye settled for a moment.

The night of union—how fast it sped past;
and the night of separation, how very burdensome it is.

Once diffused, how can the wave of fragrance be
recaptured;
once out of the heart, when has lament stayed on
the lips?

दस्त-ए-सय्याद भी आजिज़ है कफ़-ए-गुल्चीं भी
बू-ए-गुल ठहरी न बुल-बुल की ज़ुबाँ ठहरी है

आते आते यूँ ही दम भर को रुकी होगी बहार
जाते जाते यूँ ही पल भर को ख़िज़ाँ ठहरी है

हमने जो तर्ज़-ए-फ़ुग़ाँ की है क़फ़स में ईजाद
फ़ैज़ गुलशन में वही तर्ज़-ए-बयाँ ठहरी है

دستِ صیّاد بھی عاجز ہے کفِ گلچیں بھی
بوئے گل ٹھہری نہ بلبل کی زباں ٹھہری ہے

آتے آتے یوں ہی دم بھر کو رُکی ہوگی بہار
جاتے جاتے یوں ہی پل بھر کو خزاں ٹھہری ہے

ہم نے جو طرزِ فغاں کی ہے قفس میں ایجاد
فیض گلشن میں وہی طرزِ بیاں ٹھہری ہے

Helpless is the bird-killer's hand, so also the flower-
gatherer's—
nothing has stayed on, not the scent of a rose, nor
the nightingale's song.

In its smooth coming, spring must have paused for
a moment,
and in its going, stalled autumn momentarily.

The style of lament I innovated in captivity—
that mode, O Faiz, has caught on everywhere in the
garden.

आए कुछ अब्र, कुछ शराब आए
उस के बाद आए जो अज़ाब आए
बाम-ए-मीना से माहताब उतरे
दस्त-ए-साक़ी में आफ़ताब आए
हर रग-ए-ख़ूँ में फिर चराग़ाँ हो
सामने फिर वो बेनक़ाब आए
उम्र के हर वरक़ पे दिल को नज़र
तेरी मेहर-ओ-वफ़ा के बाब आए
कर रहा था ग़म-ए-जहाँ का हिसाब
आज तुम याद बेहिसाब आए
न गई तेरे ग़म की सरदारी
दिल में यूँ रोज़ इन्क़लाब आए
जल उठे बज़्म-ए-ग़ैर के दर-ओ-बाम
जब भी हम ख़ानमाँख़राब आए
इस तरह अपनी ख़ामुशी गूँजी
गोया हर सम्त से जवाब आए
फ़ैज़ थी राह सर बसर मंज़िल
हम जहाँ पहुँचे, कामयाब आए

آئے کچھ ابر، کچھ شراب آئے
اس کے بعد آئے جو عذاب آئے
بامِ مینا سے ماہتاب اترے
دستِ ساقی میں آفتاب آئے
ہر رگِ خوں میں پھر چراغاں ہو
سامنے پھر وہ بے نقاب آئے
عمر کے ہر ورق پہ دل کو نظر
تیری مہر و وفا کے باب آئے
کر رہا تھا غمِ جہاں کا حساب
آج تم یاد بے حساب آئے
نہ گئی تیرے غم کی سرداری
دل میں یوں روز انقلاب آئے
جل اٹھے بزمِ غیر کے در و بام
جب بھی ہم خانماں خراب آئے
اس طرح اپنی خامشی گونجی
گویا ہر سمت سے جواب آئے
فیض تھی راہ سر بسر منزل
ہم جہاں پہنچے، کامیاب آئے

Let There Be Some Clouds

Let there be some clouds, some wine
and then if retribution follows, who cares?

Let the moon descend to the terrace
and in the cup-bearer's palm appear the sun.

Let candles light up in every blood-vein
as she appears, her face unveiled.

On every page of the book of life, my heart saw
a sequence of the cantos of your kindness and loyalty.

Counting today the sorrows of this world—
endlessly I remembered you.

Never could I challenge your love's daily supremacy
even though revolt has been my heart's daily wont.

Up in flames went my rival's concourse—roof and
doors,
each time my destitute self showed up there.

Such was the resonance of my silence,
it seemed answers echoed from all directions.

Fully triumphant was my life's journey, O Faiz,
success greeted me wherever I went.

ज़िदाँ की एक शाम

शाम के पेचो ख़म सितारों से
ज़ीना-ज़ीना उतर रही है रात
यूँ सबा पाससे गुज़रती है
जैसे कह दी किसी ने प्यार की बात
सहने ज़िन्दाँ के बेवतन अशजार
सरनिगूँ, म्हव हैं बनाने में
दामने आसमाँ पे नक़्शो निगार
शाना-ए-बाम पर दमकता है
मेहरबाँ चाँदनी का दस्ते जमील
ख़ाक में घुल गयी है आबे नुजूम
नूर में घुल गया है अर्श का नील
सब्ज़ गोशों में नीलगूँ साये
लहलहाते हैं जिस तरह दिल में
मौजे दर्दे फ़िराक़े यार आये
दिल से पैहम ख़्याल कहता है
इतनी शीरीं है ज़िन्दगी इस पल
ज़ुल्म का ज़हर घोलने वाले
कामराँ हो सकेंगे आज न कल
जलवागाहे विसाल की शमएं
वो बुझा भी चुके अगर तो क्या
चाँद को गुल करें तो हम जानें

زنداں کی ایک شام

شام کے پیچ وخم ستاروں سے
زینہ زینہ اُتر رہی ہے رات
یوں صبا پاس سے گزرتی ہے
جیسے کہہ دی کسی نے پیار کی بات
صحنِ زنداں کے بے وطن اشجار
سرنگوں، محو ہیں بنانے میں
دامنِ آسماں پہ نقش ونگار
شانۂ بام پر دمکتا ہے
مہرباں چاندنی کا دستِ جمیل
خاک میں گھل گئی ہے آبِ نجوم
نور میں گھل گیا ہے عرش کا نیل
سبز گوشوں میں نیلگوں سائے
لہلہاتے ہیں جس طرح دل میں
موجِ دردِ فراقِ یار آئے
دل سے پیہم خیال کہتا ہے
اتنی شیریں ہے زندگی اس پل
ظلم کا زہر گھولنے والے
کامراں ہو سکیں گے آج نہ کل
جلوہ گاہِ وصال کی شمعیں
وہ بجھا بھی چکے اگر تو کیا
چاند کو گل کریں تو ہم جانیں

Prison: One Evening

From the sinuous pathways of evening stars,
the night climbs down, step by step.
From close-by, the breeze streams past
as though someone has dropped a word of love.
In the prison courtyard, the trees—exiled,
heads drooping, absorbed in embroidering the
sky's hem.
On the terrace's shoulder, blazes
benign moonlight's beautiful hand.
In the dust is dissolved the stars' lustre
and the sky's turquoise is suffused with light.
In the green niches sway blue reflections
as if the heart is swayed by the parting ache.

Ceaselessly wells up in my heart the thought—
how very sweet this instant is.
Those busy concocting poison
will succeed
neither today nor tomorrow.

What if you have put out the candles
in our luminous chamber of love—
snuff out the moon
and I'll concede defeat.

याद

दश्ते तन्हाई में, ऐ जाने जहाँ, लरज़ाँ हैं
तेरी आवाज़ के साये, तेरे होंटों के सराब
दश्ते तन्हाई में दूरी के ख़सो ख़ाक तले
खिल रहे हैं तेरे पहलू के समन और गुलाब

उठ रही है कहीं कुरबत से तेरी सांस की आंच
अपनी खुशबू में सुलगती हुई मद्धम मद्धम
दूर उफ़क़ पार, चमकती हुई क़तरा-क़तरा
गिर रही है तेरी दिलदार नज़र की शबनम

इस क़दर प्यार से, ऐ जाने जहाँ, रखा है
दिल के रुख़सार पे इस वक्त तेरी याद ने हात
यूँ गुमाँ होता है, गर्चे है अभी सुबह फ़िराक़
ढल गया हिज्र का दिन, आ भी गयी वस्ल की रात

یاد

دشتِ تنہائی میں، اے جان جہاں، لرزاں ہیں
تیری آواز کے سائے، ترے ہونٹوں کے سراب
دشت تنہائی میں دوری کے خس و خاک تلے
کِھل رہے ہیں، ترے پہلو کے سمن اور گلاب

اٹھ رہی ہے کہیں قربت سے تری سانس کی آنچ
اپنی خوشبو میں سلگتی ہوئی مدھم مدھم
دور افق پار، چمکتی ہوئی قطرہ قطرہ
گر رہی ہے تری دلدار نظر کی شبنم

اس قدر پیار سے، اے جانِ جہاں، رکھا ہے
دل کے رُخسار پہ اس وقت تری یاد نے ہات
یوں گماں ہوتا ہے، گرچہ ہے ابھی صبحِ فراق
ڈھل گیا ہجر کا دن، آ بھی گئی وصل کی رات

Remembrance

In the wilderness of my heart, O love,
waver
the shadows of your voice
the mirages of your lips.
In the desert of loneliness—
there, under the remote dust and straw of separation—
are unfolding the jasmines and roses of your lap.

There rises, from closeby, the flame of your breath
glowing softly in its own heady fragrance.
And there, beyond the horizon, falls
drop by drop, the effulgent dew
of your alluring glance.

O my love, with such tenderness
has your memory's hand caressed the cheeks
of my heart that it appears, as if,

although it is still the dawn of separation,
the day of parting has faded away
and the night of love's union has just arrived.

शाम-ए-फ़िराक़, अब न पूछ, आई और आके टल गई
दिल था के फिर बहल गया, जाँ थी के फिर सम्भल गई

बज़्म-ए-ख़्याल में तेरे हुस्न की शमा जल गई
दर्द का चाँद बुझ गया, हिज्र की रात ढल गई

जब मुझे याद कर लिया, सुबह महक-महक उठी
जब तेरा ग़म जगा लिया, रात मचल मचल गई

दिल से तो हर मुआमला करके चले थे साफ़ हम
कहने में उनके सामने बात बदल बदल गई

आख़िर-ए-शब के हमसफ़र फ़ैज़ न जाने क्या हुए
रह गई किस जगह सबा, सुबह किधर निकल गयी

شامِ فراق، اب نہ پوچھ، آئی اور آکے ٹل گئی
دل تھا کہ پھر بہل گیا، جاں تھی کہ پھر سنبھل گئی

بزمِ خیال میں ترے حسن کی شمع جل گئی
درد کا چاند بجھ گیا، ہجر کی رات ڈھل گئی

جب تجھے یاد کرلیا، صبح مہک مہک اٹھی
جب ترا غم جگالیا، رات مچل مچل گئی

دل سے تو ہر معاملہ کرکے چلے تھے صاف ہم
کہنے میں ان کے سامنے بات بدل بدل گئی

آخرِ شب کے ہم سفر فیض نہ جانے کیا ہوئے
رہ گئی کس جگہ صبا، صبح کدھر نکل گئی

Ask Me Not About the Evening of Parting

Ask me not about the evening of parting—it came and passed—
it was the heart that again felt consoled
and it was life that regained its poise.

In my fancy was kindled your beauty's fame—
gone was the moon of pain, gone the night of separation.

Whenever I remembered you, the morning came alive, fragrant
and whenever I revived your sorrow, the night went restive.

With my heart I'd already settled what to say—
but when it came to saying it there, the words veered and hedged.

Faiz, my fellow travellers of the night's last hours, what happened to them?
where did the breeze part company and where did the morning vanish?

मुलाक़ात

ये रात उस दर्द का शजर है
जो मुझसे, तुझसे अज़ीमतर है
अज़ीमतर है कि इसकी शाख़ों
में लाख मिशअल बकफ़ सितारों
के कारवाँ, घिर के खो गये हैं
हज़ार महताब, इस के साये
में अपना सब नूर, रो गये हैं
ये रात उस दर्द का शजर है
जो मुझसे तुझसे अज़ीमतर है
मगर इसी रात के शजर से
ये चँद लमहों के ज़र्द पत्ते
गिरे हैं, और तेरे गेसुओं में
उलझ के गुलनार हो गए हैं
उसी की शबनम से ख़ामुशी के
ये चँद क़तरे, तेरी जबीं पर
बरस के, हीरे पिरो गये हैं
बहुत सिया है ये रात लेकिन
इसी सियाही में रूनुमा है
वो नहरे ख़ूँ जो मेरी सदा है
इसी के साये में नूरगर है
वो मौजे ज़र जो तेरी नज़र है

ملاقات

یہ رات اُس درد کا شجر ہے
جو مجھ سے، تجھ سے عظیم تر ہے
عظیم تر ہے کہ اس کی شاخوں
میں لاکھ مشعل بکف ستاروں
کے کارواں، گھر کے کھو گئے ہیں
ہزار مہتاب، اس کے سائے
میں اپنا سب نور، رو گئے ہیں
یہ رات اُس درد کا شجر ہے
جو مجھ سے تجھ سے عظیم تر ہے
مگر اسی رات کے شجر سے
یہ چند لمحوں کے زرد پتے
گرے ہیں، اور تیرے گیسوؤں میں
الجھ کے گلنار ہو گئے ہیں
اسی کی شبنم سے خامشی کے
یہ چند قطرے، تری جبیں پر
برس کے، ہیرے پرو گئے ہیں
بہت سیہ ہے یہ رات لیکن
اسی سیاہی میں رونما ہے
وہ نہرِ خوں جو مری صدا ہے
اسی کے سائے میں نور گر ہے
وہ موجِ زر جو تری نظر ہے

Rendezvous

This night is that pain's tree
which towers higher than you or me—
higher it is, for in its boughs are lost
the caravans of a hundred thousand torch-bearing
stars;
a thousand moons have, under its shadow, wailed
over the loss of their lustre.

This night is that pain's tree
which towers higher than you or me;
but from this very tree have fallen
the pallid leaves of these few moments;
tangled in your locks, they have blossomed into
scarlet.
From this very dew have fallen
a few drops of silence on your forehead
and are now strung into pearls.

Ebony dark is the night
but truly in this darkness emerges
that river of blood which is my cry,
and just under its shadow is that illuminator,
the rich wave of gold—
your eye.

वो ग़म जो इस वक़्त तेरी बाहों
के गुलसिताँ में सुलग रहा है
(वो ग़म, जो इस रात का समर है)
कुछ और तप जाए अपनी आहों
की आंच में तो यही शरर है
हर इक सिया शाख़ की कमाँ से
जिगर में टूटे हैं तीर जितने
जिगर से नोचे हैं, और हर इक
का हमने तेशा बना लिया है
अलम नसीबों, जिगर फ़गारों
की सुबह अफ़लाक पर नहीं है
जहाँ पे हम तुम खड़ें हैं दोनों
सहर का रोशन उफ़क़ यहीं है
यहीं पे ग़म के शरार खिलकर
शफ़क़ का गुलज़ार बन गए हैं
यहीं पे क़ातिल दुखों के तेशे
क़तार अंदर क़तार किरनों
के आतशीं हार बन गये हैं
ये ग़म जो इस रात ने दिया है
ये ग़म सहर का यक़ीं बना है
यक़ीं जो ग़म से करीमतर है
सहर जो शब से अज़ीमतर है

وہ غم جو اس وقت تیری باہوں
کے گلستاں میں سُلگ رہا ہے
(وہ غم، جو اس رات کا ثمر ہے)
کچھ اور تپ جائے اپنی آہوں
کی آنچ میں تو یہی شرر ہے
ہر اک سیہ شاخ کی کماں سے
جگر میں ٹوٹے ہیں تیر جتنے
جگر سے نوچے ہیں، اور ہر اک
کا ہم نے تیشہ بنا لیا ہے
الم نصیبوں، جگر فگاروں
کی صبح، افلاک پر نہیں ہے
جہاں پہ ہم تم کھڑے ہیں دونوں
سحر کا روشن اُفق یہیں ہے
یہیں پہ غم کے شرار کِھل کر
شفق کا گلزار بن گئے ہیں
یہیں پہ قاتل دکھوں کے تیشے
قطار اندر قطار کرنوں
کے آتشیں ہار بن گئے ہیں
یہ غم جو اس رات نے دیا ہے
یہ غم سحر کا یقیں بنا ہے
یقیں جو غم سے کریم تر ہے
سحر جو شب سے عظیم تر ہے

That sorrow which is smouldering, this moment,
in the rose-garden of your arms
(that sorrow which is the night's fruition),
if tempered a little more in the fire of our sighs,
would turn into a flame.

From the bow of every dark branch,
whatever arrows have pierced my heart,
I've plucked them out, forged each into a hatchet.

The dawn of the ill-fated and the heart-broken
is not up there in the sky,
but right here where you and I stand—
here glows the bright horizon of dawn.
It is here that sorrow's sparks have blossomed
into a garden of the crimson dusk,
and this is where the hatchets of fatal afflictions
have turned, rows within rows,
into the fiery garlands of sunbeams.

This very sorrow, boon of the night,
has lent us a faith for the future—
faith, far more bountiful than pain
and dawn, far grander than night.

फ़िक्रे सूदो ज़ियाँ तो छूटेगी
मिन्ते ई-ओ-आँ तो छूटेगी
ख़ैर, दोज़ख़ में मय मिले न मिले
शेख़ साहब से जाँ तो छूटेगी

न आज लुत्फ कर इतना कि कल गुज़र न सके
वो रात जो के तेरे गेसुओं की रात नहीं
ये आरज़ू भी बड़ी चीज़ है मगर हमदम
विसाले यार फ़क़त आरज़ू की बात नहीं

فکر سود و زیاں تو چھوٹے گی
مِنّتِ ایں و آں تو چھوٹے گی
خیر، دوزخ میں مے ملے نہ ملے
شیخ صاحب سے جاں تو چھوٹے گی

نہ آج لطف کر اتنا کہ کل گزر نہ سکے
وہ رات جو کہ ترے گیسوؤں کی رات نہیں
یہ آرزو بھی بڑی چیز ہے مگر ہمدم
وصالِ یار فقط آرزو کی بات نہیں

Quatrains

At last I'll be rid of all concern for pain or loss—
also rid of the need to beseech all and sundry.
Never mind if there'll be no wine in hell—
at least the preacher will be nowhere around.

Grant me not so much bounty today that tomorrow
night, without your locks,
may become too wearisome.
Yearning is a great thing, O friend,
but union with the beloved is not just a matter of
longing.

गुलों में रंग भरे, बाद-ए-नौबहार चले
चले भी आओ कि गुलशन का कारोबार चले

گلوں میں رنگ بھرے بادِ نوبہار چلے
چلے بھی آؤ کہ گلشن کا کاروبار چلے

क़फ़स उदास है यारो सबा से कुछ तो कहो
कहीं तो बहर-ए-खुदा आज ज़िक्र-ए-यार चले

قفس اداس ہے یارو صبا سے کچھ تو کہو
کہیں تو بہرِ خدا آج ذکرِ یار چلے

कभी तो सुबह तेरे कुंज-ए-लब से हो आग़ाज़
कभी तो शब सर-ए-काकुल से मुश्कबार चले

کبھی تو صبح ترے کنجِ لب سے ہو آغاز
کبھی تو شب سرِ کاکل سے مشکبار چلے

बड़ा है दर्द का रिश्ता, ये दिल ग़रीब सही
तुम्हारे नाम पे आयेंगे ग़मगुसार चले

بڑا ہے درد کا رشتہ، یہ دل غریب سہی
تمہارے نام پہ آئیں گے غمگسار چلے

जो हम पे गुज़री सो गुज़री मगर शब-ए-हिज्राँ
हमारे अश्क तेरी आक़ेबत सँवार चले

جو ہم پہ گزری سو گزری مگر شبِ ہجراں
ہمارے اشک تری عاقبت سنوار چلے

हुज़ूर-ए-यार हुई दफ़्तर-ए-जुनूँ की तलब
गिरह में लेके गरेबाँ का तार तार चले

حضورِ یار ہوئی دفترِ جنوں کی طلب
گرہ میں لے کے گریباں کا تار تار چلے

मक़ाम, फ़ैज़, कोई राह में जचा ही नहीं
जो कू-ए-यार से निकले तो सू-ए-दार चले

مقام، فیضؔ، کوئی راہ میں جچا ہی نہیں
جو کوئے یار سے نکلے تو سوئے دار چلے

Lending Colour to the Flowers

Lending hues to the flowers, blows the
spring breeze,
Now do come to let the garden blossom.

Sad is the cage, O friends, say something to the breeze,
somewhere, for God's sake, should be some talk
of the beloved today;

let the day break from the curl of your lips
and let the night go fragrant with the crest of your
locks.

Let the heart be humble—but deep is the bond of love;
if I invoke your name, many will come to commiserate
with me.

Whatever befell me, let it be; at least my tears,
O night of separation, had surely brightened you up.

Whenever my frenzy was summoned before my
love,
I appeared, my collar in shreds, as my lone asset.

No resting place, O Faiz, appealed all through the
journey;
as I emerged from my beloved's lane, I headed straight
for the gallows.

सुबह फूटी तो आसमाँ पे तेरे
रंगे रूख़सार की फुहार गिरी
रात छाई तो रूए आलम पर
तेरी जुल्फों की आबशार गिरी

तमाम शब दिले वहशी तलाश करता है
हर इक सदा में तेरे हर्फ़े लुत्फ़ का आहंग
हर एक सुबह मिलाती है बार-बार नज़र
तेरे दहन से हर एक लाला-ओ-गुलाब का रंग

صبح پھوٹی تو آسماں پہ ترے
رنگ رخسار کی پھوہار گری
رات چھائی تو رُوئے عالم پر
تیری زلفوں کی آبشار گری

تمام شب دلِ وحشی تلاش کرتا ہے
ہر اک صدا میں ترے حرفِ لطف کا آہنگ
ہر ایک صبح ملاتی ہے بار بار نظر
ترے دہن سے ہر اک لالہ وگلاب کا رنگ

Quatrains

With the crack of dawn was sprayed in the sky
the roseate of your cheeks,
and with nightfall came down the cascade
of your tresses on the world's face.

All through the night, my wild heart craves
for you—
in every cry the harmony of your kind word.
Each morning my eye sees in your lips,
time and again, the tints of the tulip and the rose.

दरीचा

गड़ी हैं कितनी सलीबें मेरे दरीचे में
हर एक अपने मसीहा के ख़ूँ का रंग लिए
हर एक वसले खुदावंद की उमंग के लिए

किसी पे करते हैं अब्रे बहार को कुरबाँ
किसी पे क़तल महे ताबनाक करते हैं
किसी पे होती है सरमस्त शाख़सार दो नीम
किसी पे बादे सबा को हलाक करते हैं
हर आये दिन ये खुदावंदगाने मेहरो जमाल
लहू में ग़र्क़ मेरे ग़मकदे में आते हैं
और आये दिन मेरी नज़रों के सामने उनके
शहीद जिस्म सलामत उठाए जाते हैं

دریچہ

گڑی ہیں کتنی صلیبیں مرے دریچے میں
ہر ایک اپنے مسیحا کے خوں کا رنگ لئے
ہر ایک وصلِ خداوند کی اُمنگ لئے

کسی پہ کرتے ہیں ابرِ بہار کو قرباں
کسی پہ قتل مہِ تابناک کرتے ہیں
کسی پہ ہوتی ہے سرمست شاخسار دو نیم
کسی پہ بادِ صبا کو ہلاک کرتے ہیں
ہر آئے دن یہ خداوندگانِ مہر و جمال
لہو میں غرق مرے غمکدے میں آتے ہیں
اور آئے دن مری نظروں کے سامنے ان کے
شہید جسم سلامت اٹھائے جاتے ہیں

Casement

How many crosses are fixed in my casement,
each tinged with the blood of its own messiah,
each yearning for union with God:

on one is sacrificed the spring's cloud,
the other held for the murder of the bright moon.
If for one the fruit-laden bough is beheaded,
for the other is killed the morning breeze.

Each new day, these gods of grace and beauty
visit my sorrowland, soaked in blood,
and each day, right before my eyes,
are carried away their martyred bodies.

दर्द आएगा दबे पाँव

और कुछ देर में, जब फिर मेरे तन्हा दिल को
फ़िक्र आलेगी कि तन्हाई का क्या चारा करे
दर्द आएगा दबे पाँव लिए सुर्ख़ चराग़
वो जो एक दर्द धड़कता है कहीं दिल से परे

शोलए दर्द जो पहलू में लपक उठेगा
दिल की दीवार पे हर नक़्श दमक उठेगा
हलक़ए ज़ुल्फ कहीं, गोशए रुख़सार कहीं
हिज्र का दश्त कहीं, गुलशने दीदार कहीं
लुत्फ की बात कहीं, प्यार का इक़रार कहीं

दिल से फिर होगी मेरी बात कि ऐ दिल ऐ दिल
ये जो महबूब बना है तेरी तन्हाई का
ये तो मेहमाँ है घड़ी भर का चला जाएगा
उस से कब तेरी मुसीबत का मुदावा होगा

मुशतइल हो के अभी उठेंगे वहशी साये
ये चला ज़ाएगा, रह जाएंगे बाक़ी साये
रात भर जिनसे तेरा ख़ून ख़राबा होगा
जंग ठहरी है कोई खेल नहीं है ऐ दिल
दुश्मने जाँ हैं सभी, सारे के सारे क़ातिल

دردآئے گا دبے پاؤں

اور کچھ دیر میں، جب پھر مرے تنہا دل کو
فکر آلے گی کہ تنہائی کا کیا چارہ کرے
درد آے گا دبے پاؤں لئے سرخ چراغ
وہ جو اک درد دھڑکتا ہے کہیں دل سے پرے

شعلۂ درد جو پہلو میں لپک اٹھے گا
دل کی دیوار پہ ہر نقش دمک اٹھے گا
حلقۂ زلف کہیں، گوشۂ رخسار کہیں
ہجر کا دشت کہیں، گلشنِ دیدار کہیں
لطف کی بات کہیں، پیار کا اقرار کہیں

دل سے پھر ہوگی مری بات کہ اے دل اے دل
یہ جو محبوب بنا ہے تری تنہائی کا
یہ تو مہماں ہے گھڑی بھر کا چلا جائے گا
اس سے کب تیری مصیبت کا مداوا ہوگا

مشتعل ہو کے ابھی اٹھیں گے وحشی سائے
یہ چلا جائے گا' رہ جائیں گے باقی سائے
رات بھر جن سے ترا خون خرابا ہوگا
جنگ ٹھہری ہے کوئی کھیل نہیں ہے اے دل
دشمنِ جاں ہیں سبھی' سارے کے سارے قات

Pain Will Creep in Soft-footed

After a while, when my lonesome heart will once
again
be siezed by angst, how shall I cure the loneliness?
Pain will then creep in soft-footed, carrying a red
taper—
that pain which throbs beyond the heart's precincts.

As this flame will leap forth in the side,
on the heart's wall will be rekindled every mark—
somewhere a lock's whorl, somewhere a cheek's curve,
somewhere the wilderness of parting, the joy
of seeing the beloved, a kind word, or love's assent.

Then will I say, O my heart,
this thought, the beloved of your loneliness,
is only a visitant for a moment—
so how can your problem be solved?

After it's gone, will rise enraged
savage shadows, which will linger on
for me to battle with all through the night.

This is a war, O my heart, not a frolic;
all your life's enemies, all your assassins—

ये कड़ी रात भी, ये साये भी, तन्हाई भी
दर्द और जंग में कुछ मेल नहीं है ऐ दिल
लाओ, सुलगाओ कोई जोशे ग़ज़ब का इन्कार

तैश की आतिशे जर्रार कहाँ है लाओ
वो दहकता हुआ गुलज़ार कहाँ है लाओ
जिसमें गरमी भी है, हरकत भी तवानाई भी

हो न हो अपने क़बीले का भी कोई लशकर
मुन्तज़िर होगा अंधेरे की फ़सीलों के उधर

उन को शोलों के रजज़ अपना पता तो देंगे
ख़ैर, हम तक वो न पहुंचे भी, सदा तो देंगे
दूर कितनी है अभी सुबह, बता तो देंगे

یہ کڑی رات بھی، یہ سائے بھی، تنہائی بھی
درد اور جنگ میں کچھ میل نہیں ہے اے دل
لاؤ، سلگاؤ کوئی جوش غضب کا انکار

طیش کی آتش جرار کہاں ہے لاؤ
وہ دہکتا ہوا گلزار کہاں ہے لاؤ
جس میں گرمی بھی ہے، حرکت بھی توانائی بھی

ہو نہ ہو اپنے قبیلے کا بھی کوئی لشکر
منتظر ہوگا اندھیرے کی فصیلوں کے اُدھر

ان کو شعلوں کے رجز اپنا پتا تو دیں گے
خیر، ہم تک وہ نہ پہنچیں بھی، صدا تو دیں گے
دور کتنی ہے ابھی صبح، بتا تو دیں گے

this harsh night, these shadows, this loneliness.
There's nothing common between pain and war,
O my heart.
Fetch me an ember of fierce passion and kindle it,
get me from somewhere the mighty flame of wrath
with its heat, its dynamism, its puissance.

Maybe a limb of our tribe is waiting
on the other side of the ramparts of darkness.
Let's alert our comrades of our presence
through fiery martial songs.
Well, even if they don't reach us, they'll call out to us
to intimate how far the dawn still is.

रात ढलने लगी है सीनों में
आग सुलगाओ आबगीनों में
दिले उश्शाक़ की ख़बर लेना
फूल खिलते हैं इन महीनों में

आज तन्हाई किसी हमदमे दैरीं की तरह
करने आयी है मेरी साक़ीगिरी शाम ढ़ले
मुन्तज़िर बैठे हैं हम दोनों कि महताब उभरे
और तेरा अक्स झलकने लगे हर साये तले

رات ڈھلنے لگی ہے سینوں میں
آگ سُلگاؤ آبگینوں میں
دلِ عُشّاق کی خبر لینا
پھول کھلتے ہیں ان مہینوں میں

آج تنہائی کسی ہمدمِ دیریں کی طرح
کرنے آئی ہے مری ساقی گری شام ڈھلے
منتظر بیٹھے ہیں ہم دونوں کہ مہتاب ابھرے
اور ترا عکس جھلکنے لگے ہر سائے تلے

Quatrains

The night's fading away in the bosoms—
stoke up the fire in the goblet.
Take care of lovers' hearts—
these are the months for flowers to bloom.

Today loneliness, like an old friend, has come
to do some cupbearing for me, at dusk.
We're both lying in wait for the moon to rise—
and your reflections to flash in every shadow.

कोई आशिक़ किसी महबूबा से

کوئی عاشق کسی محبوبہ سے

याद की राहगुज़र जिस पे इसी सूरत से
मुद्दतें बीत गयीं हैं तुम्हें चलते-चलते
ख़त्म हो जाए जो दो-चार क़दम और चलो
मोड़ पड़ता है जहाँ दश्त-ए-फ़रामोशी का
जिसके आगे न कोई मैं हूँ न कोई तुम हो
साँस थामें हैं निगाहें, कि न जाने किस दम
तुम पलट आओ, गुज़र जाओ, या मुड़ कर देखो

یاد کی راہ گزر جس پہ اسی صورت سے
مدتیں بیت گئی ہیں تمہیں چلتے چلتے
ختم ہو جائے جو دو چار قدم اور چلو
موڑ پڑتا ہے جہاں دشتِ فراموشی کا
جس سے آگے نہ کوئی میں ہوں نہ کوئی تم ہو
سانس تھامے ہیں نگاہیں کہ نہ جانے کس دم
تم پلٹ آؤ، گزر جاؤ، یا مڑ کر دیکھو

गरचे वाक़िफ़ हैं निगाहें कि ये सब धोखा है
गर कहीं तुमसे हम-आग़ोश हुई फिर से नज़र
फूट निकलेगी वहाँ और कोई राहगुज़र
फिर इसी तरह जहां होगा मुक़ाबिल पैहम
साया-ए-ज़ुल्फ़ का और जुंबिश-ए-बाज़ू का सफ़र

گرچہ واقف ہیں نگاہیں کہ یہ سب دھوکا ہے
گر کہیں تم سے ہم آغوش ہوئی پھر سے نظر
پھوٹ نکلے گی وہاں اور کوئی راہ گزر
پھر اسی طرح جہاں ہوگا مقابل پیہم
سایہ زلف کا اور جنبشِ بازو کا سفر

दूसरी बात भी झूठी है कि दिल जानता है
याँ कोई मोड़, कोई दश्त, कोई घात नहीं
जिसके परदे में मेरा माह-ए-रवां डूब सके
तुमसे चलती रहे ये राह, यूँ ही अच्छा है
तुमने मुड़ कर भी न देखा तो कोई बात नहीं

دوسری بات بھی جھوٹی ہے کہ دل جانتا ہے
یاں کوئی موڑ کوئی دشت کوئی گھات نہیں
جس کے پردے میں مرا ماہِ رواں ڈوب سکے
تم سے چلتی رہے یہ راہ، یوں ہی اچھا ہے
تم نے مڑ کر بھی نہ دیکھا تو کوئی بات نہیں

Some Lover to His Beloved

This path of memory on which you have been trudging
for ages
if you press on a few steps further, it will wind off
to where one encounters the wilderness of oblivion,
at the bend beyond which neither I exist, nor you.
The eyes hold their breath and wonder
if you'd return, pass by, or look back.

Although the eyes know it's all an illusion
still, if they encounter you again somewhere,
a new pathway will branch out
where will begin again, as in the past,
the journey of your lock's shadow
and my outstretched arm.

The other thing is also a delusion, that the heart
knows
there's no curve, no wilderness, no ambush
behind whose screen could sink my sailing moon.
Well, it's good that this journey with you runs on;
it wouldn't matter even if you didn't look back.

तेरी उम्मीद, तेरा इंतज़ार जब से है
न शब को दिन से शिकायत न दिन को शब से है
किसी का दर्द हो करते हैं तेरे नाम रक़म
गिला है जो भी किसी से तेरे सबब से है
हुआ है जब से दिल-ए-नासबूर बेक़ाबू
कलाम तुझसे नज़र को बड़े अदब से है

अगर शरर है तो भड़के, जो फूल है तो खिले
तरह तरह की तलब तेरे रंग-ए-लब से है
कहाँ गये शब-ए-फ़ुरक़त के जागने वाले
सितारे-ए-सेहरी हम-कलाम कब से है

تری امید، ترا انتظار جب سے ہے
نہ شب کو دن سے شکایت نہ دن کو شب سے ہے
کسی کا درد ہو کرتے ہیں تیرے نام رقم
گلہ ہے جو بھی کسی سے ترے سبب سے ہے
ہوا ہے جب سے دلِ ناصبور بے قابو
کلام تجھ سے نظر کو بڑے ادب سے ہے

اگر شرر ہے تو بھڑکے، جو پھول ہے تو کھلے
طرح طرح کی طلب، تیرے رنگِ لب سے ہے
کہاں گئے شب فرقت کے جاگنے والے
ستارۂ سحری ہم کلام کب سے ہے

Ever Since I Have Been Waiting for You

Ever since I have been waiting for you,
buoyed up on hope,
neither has the night any grievance against the day
nor the day against the night.
Anybody else's pain, I attribute to you,
and you are the cause of my grudge against anyone.
Ever since my restless heart has gone out of control,
my eyes have learnt to converse with you,
deferentially.
If it's a spark, let it leap out,
if a bud, let it blossom—
diverse are my demands from your crimson lips.
Where have they gone, those who kept awake during the
night of separation—
since when has the morning-star been engaged in a
colloquy?

न दीद है न सुख़न, अब न हर्फ़ है न पयाम
कोई भी हेलाए तसकीं नहीं और आस बहुत है
उम्मीदे यार, नज़र का मिज़ाज, दर्द का रंग
तुम आज कुछ भी न पूछो कि दिल उदास बहुत है

نہ دید ہے نہ سخن، اب نہ حرف ہے نہ پیام
کوئی بھی حیلۂ تسکیں نہیں اور آس بہت ہے
امیدِ یار، نظر کا مزاج، درد کا رنگ
تم آج کچھ بھی نہ پوچھو کہ دل اداس بہت ہے

Quatrain

Not a glimpse of you—no word, no message
no ground for solace, yet hope unbounded.
Yearning for the beloved, the eye's mood, pain's
hue—don't you
ask me anything today, the heart's brimful
with despair.

शाम

इस तरह है कि हर एक पेड़ कोई मन्दिर है
कोई उजड़ा हुआ, बेनूर पुराना मंदिर
ढूंढता है जो ख़राबी के बहाने कब से
चाक हर बाम, हर एक दर का दमे आख़िर है
आसमाँ कोई पुरोहित है जो हर बाम तले
जिस्म पर राख मले, माथे पे सिन्दूर मले
सरनिगूँ बैठा है चुप चाप न जाने कब से
इस तरह है कि पसे पर्दा कोई साहिर है

जिस ने आफ़ाक़ पे फैलाया है यूँ सहर का दाम
दामने वक़्त से पेवस्त है यूँ दामने शाम
अब कभी शाम बुझेगी न अंधेरा होगा
अब कभी रात ढ़लेगी न सवेरा होगा

आसमाँ आस लिए है कि ये जादू टूटे
चुप की ज़ंजीर कटे, वक़्त का दामन छूटे
दे कोई संख दुहाई, कोई पायल बोले
कोई बुत जागे, कोई साँवली घूंघट खोले

شام

اس طرح ہے کہ ہر اک پیڑ کوئی مندر ہے
کوئی اجڑا ہوا، بے نور پرانا مندر
ڈھونڈتا ہے جو خرابی کے بہانے کب سے
چاک ہر بام، ہر اک در کا دمِ آخر ہے
آسماں کوئی پروہت ہے جو ہر بام تلے
جسم پر راکھ ملے، ماتھے پہ سیندور ملے
سرنگوں بیٹھا ہے چپ چاپ نہ جانے کب سے
اس طرح ہے کہ پسِ پردہ کوئی ساحر ہے

جس نے آفاق پہ پھیلایا ہے یوں سحر کا دام
دامنِ وقت سے پیوست ہے یوں دامنِ شام
اب کبھی شام بجھے گی نہ اندھیرا ہوگا
اب کبھی رات ڈھلے گی نہ سویرا ہوگا

آسماں آس لیے ہے کہ یہ جادو ٹوٹے
چُپ کی زنجیر کٹے، وقت کا دامن چھوٹے
دے کوئی سنکھ دہائی، کوئی پائل بولے
کوئی بُت جاگے، کوئی سانولی گھونگھٹ کھولے

Evening

It's as though each tree is a temple—
ruined, unlit, old—
seeking, for long, justification for its decadence.
Every terrace ripped apart, every door at its last breath.
The sky a priest, sits under each terrace,
body smeared with ash, forehead hued with vermilion,
head drooping, mute—nobody knows since when.
It's as though there's some conjuror behind the screen
who has flung across the sky a net of magic.
So closely linked is time's hem with that of
the evening
that it may never fade away, nor darkness
ever descend—
now this night will never pass, nor dawn ever break.

The sky is propped up on the hope that
the spell may soon be over,
the chain of silence snap,
time's hem come unstuck—
that some conch may blare out for help, some
ankle-bells speak out,
some idol come alive, some dusky beauty unveil her face.

हम ख़स्ता तनों से मोहतसबो क्या माल मनाल का पूछते हो
जो उम्र से हमने भर पाया सब सामने लाये देते हैं
दामन में है मुश्ते ख़ाक जिगर, साग़र में है ख़ूने हसरते मय
लो हमने दामन झाड़ दिया, लो जाम उलटाए देते हैं

ہم خستہ تنوں سے محتسبو کیا مال منال کا پوچھتے ہو
جو عمر سے ہم نے بھر پایا سب سامنے لائے دیتے ہیں
دامن میں ہے مشتِ خاکِ جگر، ساغر میں ہے خونِ حسرتِ مے
لو ہم نے دامن جھاڑ دیا، لو جام الٹائے دیتے ہیں

Quatrain

We are the enfeebled, what's there to ask about our
assets, O Censors.
All that life has proffered us, we're holding up
for scrutiny:
In the hem a handful of the heart's dust, in the
goblet the blood of yearning's wine
Look, here we empty our hem, and here we upturn
the wine-glass.

कब ठहरेगा दर्द-ए-दिल, कब रात बसर होगी
सुनते थे वो आयेंगे, सुनते थे सहर होगी

कब जान लहू होगी, कब अश्क गुहर होगा
किस दिन तेरी शुनवाई, ऐ दीदा-ए-तर होगी
कब महकेगी फ़सले-गुल, कब बहकेगा मयख़ाना
कब सुबह-ए-सुख़न होगी, कब शाम-ए-नज़र होगी
वाइज़ है न ज़ाहिद है, नासेह है न क़ातिल है
अब शहर में यारों की किस तरह बसर होगी
कब तक अभी रह देखें, ऐ क़ामते-जाना ना
कब हश्र मुअय्यन है तुझको तो ख़बर होगी

کب ٹھہرے گا درد اے دل کب رات بسر ہوگی
سنتے تھے وہ آئیں گے سنتے تھے سحر ہوگی

کب جان لہو ہوگی ، کب اشک گہر ہوگا
کس دن تری شنوائی اے دیدۂ تر ہوگی
کب مہکے گی فصلِ گل، کب بہکے گا میخانہ
کب صبحِ سخن ہوگی کب شامِ نظر ہوگی
واعظ ہے نہ زاہد ہے، ناصح ہے نہ قاتل ہے
اب شہر میں یاروں کی کس طرح بسر ہوگی
کب تک ابھی رہ دیکھیں اے قامتِ جانانہ
کب حشر معین ہے تجھ کو تو خبر ہوگی

When Will Pain Cease?

When will pain cease, O heart, when will the night
pass away?
It was rumoured that she'd come; and it would soon
be dawn.

When will life turn into blood, and tears become
pearls?
And when will you be heard, O my tearful eye?

When will the flowers bloom, and when will the
tavern go heady?
When will morning inspire verse, and when will
evening bring us together?

No preacher, no ascetic, no counsellor, no assassin—
how will it now fare with the lovers in town?

How long will I keep looking for you, O my beloved?
When is that doomsday ordained, surely you'd know.

बेदम हुए बीमार दवा क्यों नहीं देते
तुम अच्छे मसीहा हो शिफ़ा क्यों नहीं देते

بے دم ہوئے بیمار دوا کیوں نہیں دیتے
تم اچھے مسیحا ہو، شفا کیوں نہیں دیتے

दर्दे-शबे-हिज्रां की जज़ा क्यों नहीं देते
खूने-दिले-वहशी का सिला क्यों नहीं देते

دردِ شبِ ہجراں کی جزا کیوں نہیں دیتے
خونِ دلِ وحشی کا صِلا کیوں نہیں دیتے

मिट जाएगी मख़लूक़ तो इन्साफ करोगे
मुन्सिफ़ हो तो अब हश्र उठा क्यों नहीं देते

مٹ جائے گی مخلوق تو انصاف کروگے
منصف ہو تو اب حشر اٹھا کیوں نے دیتے

हां नुक्ता-वरो लाओ लबो-दिल की गवाही
हाँ नग़मागरो साज़े-सदा क्यों नहीं देते

ہاں نکتہ ورو لاؤ لب و دل کی گواہی
ہاں نغمہ گرو سازِ صدا کیوں نہیں دیتے

पैमाने-जुनूं हाथों को शरमाएगा कब तक
दिलवालों गिरेबाँ का पता क्यों नहीं देते

پیمانِ جنوں ہاتھوں کو شرمائے گا کب تک
دل والو، گریباں کا پتا کیوں نہیں دیتے

बरबादिए-दिल जब्र नहीं फ़ैज़ किसी का
वो दुश्मने-जां है तो भुला क्यों नहीं देते

بربادئ دل جبر نہیں فیض کسی کا
وہ دشمنِ جاں ہے تو بھلا کیوں نہیں دیتے

This Patient Breathless

This patient breathless, why don't you reclaim him?
A strange messiah are you, why don't you cure him?
Why is there no recompense for the aching night
of separation?
Why is there no reward for the sacrifice of love's
frenzy?
Will you dispense justice after mankind is
wiped out?
If you are a true judge, why not proclaim
doomsday today?
Call in the scar of pain, you discerners,
to bring up the testimony of speech and feeling,
and you music-makers, why don't you strike up
the song?
How long will frenzy's vow hold back its hand?
O lovers, why don't you point to the collar torn?
O Faiz, nobody compels you to endure the
heart's ravage;
if she's your heart's enemy, why don't you forget her?

ख़त्म हुई बारिशे संग

नागहाँ आज मेरे तार-ए-नज़र से कट कर
टुकड़े-टुकड़े हुए आफ़ाक़ पे ख़ुरशीदो-क़मर
अब किसी सम्त अंधेरा न उजाला होगा
बुझ गयी दिल की तरह राहे वफ़ा मेरे बाद
दोस्तो! क़ाफिला ऐ दर्द का क्या होगा अब

अब कोई और करे परवरिशे गुलशने-ग़म
दोस्तो ख़त्म हुई दीद-ए तर की शबनम
थम गया शोरे जुनूँ ख़त्म हुई बारिशे संग
ख़ाके रह आज लिए है लबे दिलदार का रंग
कूए जानाँ में खुला मेरे लहू का परचम
देखिए देते हैं किस-किस को सदा मेरे बाद
"कौन होता है हरीफ़े मये मरदाफ़गने इश्क़
है मुकर्रर लबे साक़ी पे सला मेरे बाद"

ختم ہوئی بارشِ سنگ

ناگہاں آج مرے تارِ نظر سے کٹ کر
ٹکڑے ٹکڑے ہوئے آفاق پہ خورشید و قمر
اب کسی سمت اندھیرا نہ اجالا ہوگا
بجھ گئی دل کی طرح راہِ وفا میرے بعد
دوستو! قافلۂ درد کا اب کیا ہوگا

اب کوئی اور کرے پرورشِ گلشنِ غم
دوستو ختم ہوئی دیدۂ تر کی شبنم
تھم گیا شورِ جنوں ختم ہوئی بارشِ سنگ
خاکِ رہ آج لئے ہے لبِ دلدار کا رنگ
کوئے جاناں میں کھلا میرے لہو کا پرچم
دیکھیے دیتے ہیں کس کس کو صدا میرے بعد
"کون ہوتا ہے حریفِ مئے مرد افگنِ عشق
ہے مکرر لبِ ساقی پہ صلا میرے بعد"

End of the Rain of Stones

Suddenly, today, sundered from my vision's thread,
lay splintered in the sky the sun and the moon.
Now there'll be no light or darkness anywhere.
Extinguished, after me, like the heart, is the path of
commitment—
friends, how will it now fare with the caravan of pain?

Let somebody else now nurture the garden of sorrow;
friends, now has dried up the dew of the grieving eye,
now stalled frenzy's uproar, the rain of stones.
Today the pathway's dust carried the tint of the
beloved's lips,
and there stands unfurled, in her lane, the banner of
my blood.
Let's see which ones will be called out after I'm gone—
'Let's see who stands up to the fatal intoxication
of love,
for I still hear, from the cupbearer, the call for another
round, after I'm gone.'

कहाँ जाओगे?

और कुछ देर में लुट जाएगा हर बाम पे चाँद
अक्स खो जाएँगे, आईने तरस जाएँगे
अर्श के दीदा-ए नमनाक से बारी-बारी
सब सितारे सरे ख़ाशाक बरस जाएँगे
आस के मारे थके हारे शबिस्तानों में
अपनी तन्हाई समेटेगा, बिछाएगा कोई
बेवफ़ाई की घड़ी, तर्के मदारात का वक़्त
इस घड़ी अपने सिवा याद न आएगा कोई
तर्के दुनिया का समाँ, ख़त्मे मुलाक़ात का वक़्त
इस घड़ी ऐ दिले आवारा कहाँ जाओगे
इस घड़ी कोई किसी का भी नहीं, रहने दो
कोई इस वक़्त मिलेगा ही नहीं, रहने दो
और मिलेगा भी तो इस तौर कि पछताओगे
इस घड़ी ऐ दिले आवारा कहाँ जाओगे
और कुछ देर ठहर जाओ कि फिर नश्तरे सुबह
ज़ख़्म की तरह हर एक आँख को बेदार करे
और हर कुश्ताए दामाँदगीए आख़िरे शब
भूल कर साअते दरमाँदगीए आख़िरे शब
जान पहचान मुलाक़ात पे इसरार करे

کہاں جاؤ گے ؟

اور کچھ دیر میں لٹ جائے گا ہر بام پہ چاند
عکس کھو جائیں گے، آئینے ترس جائیں گے
عرش کے دیدۂ نمناک سے باری باری
سب ستارے سرِ خاشاک برس جائیں گے
آس کے مارے تھکے ہارے شبستانوں میں
اپنی تنہائی سمیٹے گا، بچھائے گا کوئی
بے وفائی کی گھڑی، ترکِ مدارات کا وقت
اس گھڑی اپنے سوا یاد نہ آئے گا کوئی
ترکِ دنیا کا سماں، ختمِ ملاقات کا وقت
اس گھڑی اے دلِ آوارہ کہاں جاؤ گے
اس گھڑی کوئی کسی کا بھی نہیں، رہنے دو
کوئی اس وقت ملے گا ہی نہیں، رہنے دو
اور ملے گا بھی تو اس طور کہ پچھتاؤ گے
اس گھڑی اے دلِ آوارہ کہاں جاؤ گے
اور کچھ دیر ٹھہر جاؤ کہ پھر نشترِ صبح
زخم کی طرح ہر اک آنکھ کو بیدار کرے
اور ہر کشتۂ واماندگیِ آخرِ شب
بھول کر ساعتِ درماندگیِ آخرِ شب
جان پہچان ملاقات پہ اصرار کرے

Where Will You Go?

In just a short while, the moon will be robbed
on every terrace; reflections will fade away,
mirrors look insatiated; and from the sky's moist eye
will drop down on the dust all the stars, one by one.
In the jaded chambers of hope,
someone will fold up his loneliness, another spread
it out.
This is the moment of betrayal,
of brashness—this moment when
you'll be able to remember nobody else but yourself.
This is the mood for renouncing the world—
the moment of rendezvous' end.
Where will you go this moment, O my vagrant heart?
This moment, nobody is anybody's friend—so let it be;
nor will you meet anyone now—so let it be;
and even if you do, you will only regret it.

Hold back a little longer then, till dawn's lancet
opens up, like a wound, each eye
and every victim of the fatigue of the night's end
will insist on a friendly meeting,
forgetting the night's distress.

जब तेरी समंदर आँखों में

ये धूप किनारा, शाम ढले
मिलते हैं दोनों वक़्त जहाँ
जो रात न दिन, जो आज न कल
पल भर को अमर, पल भर में धुआँ
इस धूप किनारे, पल दो पल
होटों की लपक
बाहों की छनक
ये मेल हमारा, झूठ न सच
क्यों ज़ार करो, क्यों दोष धरो
किस कारण झूठी बात करो
जब तेरी समन्दर आँखों में
इस शाम का सूरज डूबेगा
सुख सोयेंगे घर-दर वाले
और राही अपनी रह लेगा

جب تیری سمندر آنکھوں میں

یہ دھوپ کنارا، شام ڈھلے
ملتے ہیں دونوں وقت جہاں
جو رات نہ دن، جو آج نہ کل
پل بھر کو امر، پل بھر میں دھواں
اس دھوپ کنارے، پل دو پل
ہونٹوں کی لپک
باہوں کی چھنک
یہ میل ہمارا، جھوٹ نہ سچ
کیوں زار کرو، کیوں دوش دھرو
کس کارن جھوٹی بات کرو
جب تیری سمندر آنکھوں میں
اس شام کا سوج ڈوبے گا
سکھ سوئیں گے گھر در والے
اور راہی اپنی رہ لے گا

In Your Ocean Eyes

The fringe of day, dusk
where the two hours of time meet—
neither night nor day, neither today nor tomorrow.
One moment eternal, another just smoke—
on this day's fringe, for a moment or two
the fervour of lips,
the ardour of arms,
this union of ours, neither true nor false.
Why say a false thing
when in your ocean eyes
will sink this evening's sun?
Then everyone will sleep blissfully in his house
and the traveller will wend his way.

रंग है दिल का मेरे

तुम न आये थे तो हर चीज़ वही थी कि जो है
आसमां हद्दे-नज़र, राहगुज़र शीशाएमय
और अब शीशाएमय, राहगुज़र, रंगे फ़लक
रंग है दिल का मेरे "खूने-जिगर होने तक"
चम्पई रंग कभी राहते-दीदार का रंग
सुर्मई रंग की है साअते-बेज़ार का रंग
ज़र्द पत्तों का, ख़सो-ख़ार का रंग
सुर्ख़ फूलों का, दहकते हुए गुलज़ार का रंग
ज़हर का रंग, लहू रंग, शबे-तार का रंग
आसमां, राहगुज़र, शीशा-ए-मय
कोई भीगा हुआ दामन, कोई दुखती हुई रग
कोई हर लहज़ा बदलता हुआ आईना है

अब जो आये हो तो ठहरो कि कोई रंग, कोई रुत, कोई शै
एक जगह पर ठहरे
फिर से एक बार हर एक चीज़ वहीं हो कि जो है
आसमां हद्दे-नज़र, राहगुज़र राहगुज़र, शीशा-ए-मय-शीशा-ए-मय

رنگ ہے دل کا مرے

تم نہ آئے تھے تو ہر چیز وہی تھی کہ جو ہے
آسماں حدِ نظر، راہگزر' شیشۂ مے شیشۂ مے
اور اب شیشۂ مے، راہگزر' رنگ فلک،
رنگ ہے دل کا مرے "خون جگر ہونے تک"
چمپئی رنگ کبھی راحتِ دیدار کا رنگ
سرمئی رنگ کہ ہے ساعتِ بیزار کا رنگ
زرد پتوں کا، خس وخار کا رنگ
سرخ پھولوں کا دہکتے ہوئے گلزار کا رنگ
زہر کا رنگ، لہو رنگ، شبِ تار کا رنگ
آسماں، راہگزر، شیشۂ مے،
کوئی بھیگا ہوا دامن، کوئی دکھتی ہوئی رگ
کوئی ہر لحظہ بدلتا ہوا آئینہ ہے

اب جو آئے ہو تو ٹھہرو کہ کوئی رنگ' کوئی رت، کوئی شئے
ایک جگہ پر ٹھہرے
پھر سے اک بار ہر اک چیز وہی ہو کہ جو ہے
آسماں حدِ نظر، راہگزر راہگزر، شیشۂ مے شیشۂ مے

The Colour of the Moment

Before you came, everything was what it is—
the sky, vision-bound
the pathway, the wine-glass.
And now the wine-glass, the pathway, the sky's tint—
everything bears the colour of my heart
till all melts into blood.
Sometimes the golden tinge, sometimes the hue of the
joy of seeing you
sometimes ashen, the shade of the dreary moment—
the colour of yellow leaves, of thorn and trash,
of the crimson petals of the flower-beds aglow,
the tint of poison, of blood, of sable night.
The sky, the pathway, the wine-glass—
some tear-stained robe, some wincing nerve,
some ever-revolving mirror.

Now that you're here, stay on
so that some colour, some season, some object
may come to rest
and once again everything may become what it was—
the sky, vision-bound, the pathway, the wine-glass.

पास रहो

तुम मेरे पास रहो
मेरे क़ातिल, मेरे दिलदार, मेरे पास रहो
जिस घड़ी रात चले
आसमानों का लहू पी के सियह राते चले
मर्हम-ए-मुश्क लिये नश्तर-ए-अल्मास लिए
बैन करती हुई, हँसती हुई, गाती निकले
दर्द के कासनी पाज़ेब बजाती निकले
जिस घड़ी सीनों में डूबे हुये दिल
आस्तीनों में निहाँ हाथों की रह तकने लगें
आस लिये
और बच्चों के बिलकने की तरह कुल कुल-ए-मय
बहर-ए-नासुदगी मचले तो मनाये न मने
जब कोई बात बनाये न बने
जब न कोई बात चले
जिस घड़ी रात चले
जिस घड़ी मातमी, सुनसान, सियह रात चले
पास रहो
मेरे क़ातिल, मेरे दिलदार, मेरे पास रहो

پاس رہو

تم مرے پاس رہو
میرے قاتل، مرے دلدار، مرے پاس رہو
جس گھڑی رات چلے
آسمانوں کا لہو پی کے سیہ رات چلے
مرہمِ مشک لئے، نشترِ الماس لئے
بین کرتی ہوئی، ہنستی ہوئی، گاتی نکلے
درد کے کاسنی پازیب بجاتی نکلے
جس گھڑی سینوں میں ڈوبے ہوئے دل،
آستینوں میں نہاں، ہاتھوں کی رہ تکنے لگیں
آس لئے
اور بچوں کے بلکنے کی طرح قلقلِ مے
بہرِ ناسودگی مچلے تو منائے نہ منے
جب کوئی بات بنائے نہ بنے
جب نہ کوئی بات چلے
جس گھڑی رات چلے
جس گھڑی ماتمی، سنسان، سیہ رات چلے
پاس رہو
مرے قاتل، مرے دلدار، مرے پاس رہو

Stay With Me

Stay with me—
my assassin, my sweetheart—stay on.
When the night moves on
after drinking the sky's blood,
when this dark night moves on
holding musk-balm,
diamond lancet.
Wailing, laughing, singing, it moves on—
jingling the purple anklets of pain.
When hearts sunk in bosoms
wait hopefully for hands
cloaked in sleeves,
and the wine gurgles like children's whining
when their desire once aroused,
no consoling will appease

when every word spoken fails to get across,
and no word gets moving forward,
when the night spins on,
when the mournful, dreary, dark night creeps on—
stay with me,
my assassin, my sweetheart, stay on.

दीदाए तर ये वहाँ कौन नज़र करता है
कासाए-चश्म में खुँ नाबे जिगर लेके चलो
अब अगर जाओ पये अर्ज़े तलब उनके हुज़ूर
दस्तो कशकौल नहीं कासए-सर लेके चलो

दीवारे शब और अक्से रुख़े यार सामने
फिर दिल के आईने से लहू फूटने लगा
फिर वज़ए एहतियात से धुंधला गयी नज़र
फिर ज़ब्ते आरज़ू से बदन टूटने लगा

دیدۂ تر پہ وہاں کون نظر کرتا ہے
کاسۂ چشم میں خوں نابِ جگر لے کے چلو
اب اگر جاؤ پۓ عرض وطلب ان کے حضور
دست وکشکول نہیں کاسۂ سر لے کے چلو

دیوارِ شب اور عکس رخ یار سامنے
پھر دل کے آئینے سے لہو پھوٹنے لگا
پھر وضعِ احتیاط سے دھندلا گئی نظر
پھر ضبطِ آرزو سے بدن ٹوٹنے لگا

Quatrains

Who takes notice of the moist eye, there?
So go there, carrying in the eye's cup the heart's
red blood.
Now if you go there with some entreaty, some craving,
carry not a beggar's but your skull's bowl.

The night's wall, and there in front the beloved's face
reflected;
blood has again started oozing from the heart's mirror;
again has caution blurred the gaze;
the body aches again from the muzzling of desire.

यहाँ से शहर को देखो!

यहाँ से शहर को देखो तो हलक़ा हलक़ा
खिंची है जेल की सूरत हर एक सम्त फ़सील
हर एक राह गुज़र गर्दिशे असीराँ है
ना संगे मील, न मंजिल, न मुख़लिसी की सबील
जो कोई तेज़ चले रह तो पूछता है ख़्याल
कि टोकने कोई ललकार क्यों नहीं आयी?
जो कोई हाथ हिलाये तो व्हम को है सवाल
कोई छनक, कोई झंकार क्यों नहीं आई?
यहाँ से शहर को देखो तो सारी ख़लक़त में
न कोई साहबे तमकीं, न कोई वालिए होश
हर एक मर्दे जवाँ मुजरिमे-रसन ब गुलू
हर एक हसीना-ए रअना, कनीज़े हलक़ा बगौश
जो साए दूर चराग़ों के गिर्द लज़ाँ है
न जाने महफिले ग़म है कि बज़्मे जामो-सुबू
जो रंग हर दरो दीवार पर परेशाँ हैं
यहाँ से कुछ नहीं खुलता ये फूल हैं कि लहू

یہاں سے شہر کو دیکھو!

یہاں سے شہر کو دیکھو تو حلقہ در حلقہ
کھنچی ہے جیل کی صورت ہر ایک سمت فصیل
ہر ایک راہ گزر گردشِ اسیراں ہے
نہ سنگ میل، نہ منزل، نہ مخلصی کی سبیل
جو کوئی تیز چلے رہ تو پوچھتا ہے خیال
کہ ٹوکنے کوئی للکار کیوں نہیں آئی ؟
جو کوئی ہاتھ ہلائے تو وہم کو ہے سوال
کوئی چھنک، کوئی جھنکار کیوں نہیں آئی ؟
یہاں سے شہر کو دیکھو تو ساری خلقت میں
نہ کوئی صاحبِ تمکیں، نہ کوئی والئ ہوش
ہر ایک مردِ جواں مجرم رسن بہ گلو
ہر اک حسینۂ رعنا، کنیز حلقہ بگوش
جو سائے دور چراغوں کے گرد لرزاں ہیں
نہ جانے محفل غم ہے کہ بزم جام وسُبو
جو رنگ ہر درو دیوار پر پریشاں ہیں
یہاں سے کچھ نہیں کھلتا یہ پھُول ہیں کہ لہو

Look at the City from Here!

If you look at the city from here, you see
circles within circles;
every rampart like that of a prison
and every pathway a prisoner's circular walk—
no milestone, no destination, no way out.

If anyone walks fast, fancy asks:
why hasn't someone shouted to stop him?
And if somebody waves his hand, a doubt nags:
why hasn't anyone heard a chain clank?

If you look at the city from here, you'd realize
that in the entire crowd, there's nobody really
dignified,
nobody truly sagacious; every young man's neck
in a noose,
every woman a branded slave.

The shadows which waver round the distant lamps—
who knows if it's an assembly of grieving or
carousing men,
and all those hues which appear scattered on every
door and wall—
seen from here it could be the blood or flowers.

ब्लैक आउट

जब से बे नूर हुई है शमाएँ
ख़ाक में ढूंढता फिरता हूँ न जाने किस जा
खो गयी हैं मेरी दोनों आँखें
तुम जो वाक़िफ़ हो बताओ कोई पहचान मेरी
इस तरह है कि हर एक रग में उतर आया है
मौज दर मौज किसी ज़हर का क़ातिल दरिया
तेरा अरमान, तेरी याद लिये जान मेरी
जाने किस मौज में ग़लताँ है कहाँ दिल मेरा
एक पल ठहरो कि उस पार किसी दुनिया से
बर्क़ आये मेरी जानिब, यदे बयज़ा ले कर
और मेरी आँखों के गुमगश्ता गुहर
जामे ज़ुलमत से स्याह मस्त
नयी आँखों के शबे ताब गुहर
लौटा दे
एक पल ठहरो कि दरिया का कहीं पाट लगे
और नया दिल मेरा
ज़हर में धुल के फ़ना होके
किसी घाट लगे
फिर पये नज़र नये दीदाओ दिले के चलूँ
हुस्न की मदह करूँ, शौक़ का मज़मून लिखूँ

بلیک آؤٹ

جب سے بے نور ہوئی ہیں شمعیں
خاک میں ڈھونڈتا پھرتا ہوں نہ جانے کس جا
کھو گئی ہیں میری دونوں آنکھیں
تم جو واقف ہو بتاؤ کوئی پہچان مری
اس طرح ہے کہ ہر اک رگ میں اتر آیا ہے
موج در موج کسی زہر کا قاتل دریا
تیرا ارمان، تری یاد لئے جان مری
جانے کس موج میں غلطاں ہے کہاں دل میرا
ایک پل ٹھہرو کہ اس پار کسی دنیا سے
برق آئے مری جانب، ید بیضا لے کر
اور مری آنکھوں کے گم گشتہ گہر
جامِ ظلمت سے سیہ مست
نئی آنکھوں کے شب تاب گہر
لوٹا دے
ایک پل ٹھہرو کہ دریا کا کہیں پاٹ لگے
اور نیا دل میرا
زہر میں دھل کے فنا ہو کے
کسی گھاٹ لگے
پھر پئے نذر نئے دیدہ و دل لے کے چلوں
حسن کی مدح کروں، شوق کا مضمون لکھوں

Blackout

Since the lamps have been snuffed out
I have been seeking in the dust:
somewhere I've lost both my eyes.
Since you know me, tell me some mark of my being.
It's as if into every vein has seeped
some lethal river of poison, wave after wave.
With my yearning for you, and remembrance,
O my love,
I wonder in which wave my heart has been wallowing.

Hold on for a moment, for
from across some world will flash toward me
lightning, with a luminous hand,
bringing back to me the lost pearls of my eyes
drunk on the cup of darkness—
my new night-illumining eyes.

Just hold on for a while so that
somewhere the river spreads itself out
and my nascent heart, abluted in poison, will perish
to resurrect itself and touch some wharf.
Then again will I set out, with the offering of a
new heart,
a new vision, to raise a hymn to beauty
and versify passion.

सोचने दो

एक ज़रा सोचने दो
इस ख़्याबाँ में
जो इस लहज़ा बयाबाँ भी नहीं
कौन-सी शाख़ में फूल आये थे सब से पहले
कौन बे रंग हुई रंजो-तअब से पहले
और अब से पहले

किस घड़ी कौन से मौसम में यहाँ
ख़ून का क़हत पड़ा
गुल की शहे रग पे कड़ा
वक़्त पड़ा
सोचने दो
एक ज़रा सोचने दो
ये भरा शहर जो अब वादिए वीराँ भी नहीं
उसमें किस वक़्त कहाँ
आग लगी थी पहले
उस के सफबस्ता दरीचों में से किसमे अव्वल
ज़ह हुयी सुर्ख़ शुआओं की कमाँ
किस जगह जोत जगी थी पहले
सोचने दो
हम से उस देस का तुम नामो निशाँ पूछते हो

سوچنے دو

اک ذرا سوچنے دو
اس خیاباں میں
جو اس لحظہ بیاباں بھی نہیں
کون سی شاخ میں پھول آئے تھے سب سے پہلے
کون بے رنگ ہوئی رنج وتعب سے پہلے
اور اب سے پہلے

کس گھڑی کون سے موسم میں یہاں
خون کا قحط پڑا
گل کی شہ رگ پہ کڑا
وقت پڑا
سوچنے دو
اک ذرا سوچنے دو
یہ بھرا شہر جو اب وادئ ویراں بھی نہیں
اس میں کس وقت کہاں
آگ لگی تھی پہلے
اس کے صف بستہ دریچوں میں سے کس میں اول
زہ ہوئی سرخ شعاعوں کی کماں
کس جگہ جوت جگی تھی پہلے
سوچنے دو
ہم سے اُس دیس کا تم نام ونشاں پوچھتے ہو

Let Me Think

Let me think, just awhile—
in this garden
which at this moment is not even a wilderness,
on which bough sprouted the primal flowers
and which flower first blanched
with grief and fatigue?
And before this—
at which moment, and during which season
were we struck with the drought of blood
and the flower's jugular vein smarted
under time's harshness—
let me think.

Let me think a little.
This teeming city, now not even a
desolate valley—
here, when and where
did the first fire break out;
in which one of its arrayed windows
was first born the arc of blood-drenched flames—
and where did the first light flash?
Let me think.

You ask me the whereabouts of that country

जिसकी तारीख़ न जुग़राफ़िया अब याद आये
और याद आये तो महबूबे गुज़िश्ता की तरह
रूबरू आने से जी घबराए
हाँ मगर जैसे कोई
ऐसे महबूब या महबूबा का दिल रखने को
आ निकलता है कभी रात बिताने के लिए
हम भी इस उम्र को आ पहुंचे हैं जब हम भी यूँ ही
दिल से मिल आते हैं बस रस्म निभाने के लिए
दिल की क्या पूछते हो
सोचने दो

جس کی تاریخ نہ جغرافیہ اب یاد آے
اور یاد آئے تو محبوبِ گزشتہ کی طرح
روبرو آنے سے جی گھبرائے
ہاں مگر جیسے کوئی
ایسے محبوب یا محبوبہ کا دل رکھنے کو
آنکلتا ہے کبھی رات بتانے کے لئے
ہم اب اس عمر کو آ پہنچے ہیں جب ہم بھی یوں ہی
دل سے مل آتے ہیں بس رسم نبھانے کے لئے
دل کی کیا پوچھتے ہو
سوچنے دو

whose history and geography now elude my memory
and, if at all recalled somehow,
it's like a beloved of the past
encountering whom, face to face,
the heart feels unnerved—

but yes, as if someone
just to cheer up his lover,
shows up sometime to spend the night.

I have now reached that point
when even if I go over to meet my beloved
it will be just for ritual's sake.

What's there to ask of my heart?—
let me think!

हार्ट अटैक

दर्द इतना था कि उस रात दिले वहशी ने
हर रगे जाँ से उलझना चाहा
हर बुने मू से टपकना चाहा
और कहीं दूर तेरे सहने चमन में गोया
पत्ता पत्ता मेरे अफ़सुर्दा लहू में धुल कर
हुस्ने महताब से आज़ुर्दा नज़र आने लगा
मेरे वीरानए तन में गोया
सारे दुखते हुए रेशों की तनाबें खुल कर
सिलसिलेवार पता देने लगीं
रुख़सतें-क़ाफ़लए-शौक़ की तय्यारी का
और जब याद की बुझती हुई शमओं में नज़र आया कहीं
एक पुल आख़री लम्हा तेरी दिलदारी का
दर्द इतना था कि उससे भी गुज़रना चाहा
हमने चाहा भी, मगर दिल न ठहरना चाहा

ہارٹ اٹیک

درد اتنا تھا کہ اس رات دلِ وحشی نے
ہر رگِ جاں سے الجھنا چاہا
ہر بنِ مُو سے ٹپکنا چاہا
اور کہیں دور ترے صحن چمن میں گویا
پتا پتا مرے افسردہ لہو میں دھل کر
حسن مہتاب سے آزردہ نظر آنے لگا
میرے ویرانۂ تن میں گویا
سارے دکھتے ہوئے ریشوں کی طنابیں کھل کر
سلسلہ وار پتہ دینے لگیں
رخصتِ قافلہ شوق کی تیاری کا
اور جب یاد کی بجھتی ہوئی شمعوں میں نظر آیا کہیں
ایک پل آخری لمحہ تری دلداری کا
درد اتنا تھا کہ اس سے بھی گذرنا چاہا
ہم نے چاہا بھی، مگر دل نہ ٹھہرنا چاہا

Heart Attack

Pain so intense that night, my savage heart
wanted to grapple with every artery,
and drip from every pore,

and out there, as though in your courtyard,
each leaf, bathed in my despondent blood,
began to look pale in the moonlight.

In my body's desert places, it seemed
as if, all the fibres of my wincing veins, undone,
began shooting out signals, ceaselessly—
preparations for the departure of love's caravan.

And when, in memory's fading lights,
there emerged somewhere before the eye,
one last moment of your love's kindness—
the pain was so lacerating that
it ventured to overstep the moment.
I too willed to hold on to it,
but the heart would not agree.

ज़ब्त का अहद भी है शौक़ का पैमान भी है
अहदो पयमाँ से गुज़र जाने को जी चाहता है
दर्द इतना है कि हर रग में है महशर बरपा
और सुकूँ ऐसा कि मर जाने को जी चाहता है

ضبط کا عہد بھی ہے شوق کا پیمان بھی ہے
عہد و پیماں سے گزر جانے کو جی چاہتا ہے
درد اتنا ہے کہ ہر رگ میں ہے محشر برپا
اور سکوں ایسا کہ مر جانے کو جی چاہتا ہے

Quatrain

My vow of restraint, also my desire's covenant.
But I wish to move beyond both pledges and promises.
Pain so intense, there's a riot in every vein—
and such tranquility that I'd rather cease to be.

बालों पे कहीं रात ढल रही है
या शम्आ पिघल रही है
पहलू में कोई चीज़ जल रही है
तुम हो कि मेरी जाँ निकल रही है

एक सुख़न मुतरिबे ज़ेबा कि सुलग उठे बदन
एक क़दहे साक़ी महवश जो करे होश तमाम
ज़िक्रे सुबह कि रुख़े यार से रंगी था चमन
यादे शबहा कि तने यार था आग़ोश तमाम

بالوں پہ کہیں رات ڈھل رہی ہے
یا شمع پگھل رہی ہے
پہلو میں کوئی چیز جل رہی ہے
تم ہو کہ مری جاں نکل رہی ہے

اک سخن مطربِ زیبا کہ سلگ اٹھے بدن
اک قدح ساقی مہوش جو کرے ہوش تمام
ذکرِ صبح کہ رخِ یار سے رنگیں تھا چمن
یادِ شبہا کہ تنِ یار تا آغوش تمام

Somewhere Near the Pillow

Somewhere near the pillow, the night's fading away
or is it the candle melting?
Something is burning within me—
is that your memory, or my life
seeking to depart.

A verse from an enchanting singer that sets the
body afire—
a bowl of wine from an alluring cupbearer that may
turn your head;
a mention of the morning when the beloved's face lent
its colour to the garden;
the memory of the night when your beloved was
in your arms.

तब-ब-तह दिल की कदूरत
मेरी आँखों में उमड़ आयी तो कुछ चारा न था
चारागर की मान ली
और मैंने गर्द आलूद आँखों को लहू से धो लिा
मैंने गर्द आलूद आँखों को लहू से धो लिया
और अब हर शक्लो-सूरत
आलमे मौजूद की हर एक शय
मेरी आँखों के लहू से इस तरह हमरंग है
ख़ुरशीद का कुंदन लहू
महताब की चाँदी लहू
सुबहों का हंसना भी लहू
रातों का रोना भी लहू
हर शजर मीनारे ख़ूँ, हर फूल ख़ूनी दीदा है
हर नज़र एक तारे ख़ूँ, हर अक्स ख़ूँ मालीदा है
मौजे ख़ूँ जब तक रवाँ रहती है उसका सुर्ख़ रंग
जज़्बए शौक़े शहादत, दर्द, ग़ैज़ो-ग़म का रंग
और थम जाए तो कुजला कर
फ़क़त नफरत का, शब का, मौत का
हर रंग के मातम का रंग
चारागर ऐसा न होने दे
कहीं से ला कोई सैलाबे अश्क
आबे वुज़ु
जिस में धुल जाएँ तो शायद धुल सके
मेरी आँखों, मेरी गर्द आलूद आँखों का लहु

تہ بہ تہ دل کی کدورت
میری آنکھوں میں امنڈ آئی تو کچھ چارہ نہ تھا
چارہ گر کی مان لی
اور میں نے گرد آلود آنکھوں کو لہو سے دھولیا
میں نے گرد آلود آنکھوں کو لہو سے دھولیا
اور اب ہر شکل و صورت
عالم موجود کی ہر ایک شئے
میرے آنکھوں کے لہو سے اس طرح ہم رنگ ہے
خورشید کا کندن لہو
مہتاب کی چاندی لہو
صبحوں کا ہنسنا بھی لہو
راتوں کا رونا بھی لہو
ہر شجر مینارِ خوں، ہر پھول خونیں دیدہ ہے
ہر نظر اک تارِ خوں، ہر عکس خوں مالیدہ ہے
موج خوں جب تک رواں رہتی ہے اس کا سرخ رنگ
جذبۂ شوقِ شہادت، درد غیظ و غم کا رنگ
اور تھم جائے تو کجلا کر
فقط نفرت کا، شب کا، موت کا
ہر اک رنگ کے ماتم کا رنگ
چارہ گر ایسا نہ ہونے دے
کہیں سے لا کوئی سیلابِ اشک
آبِ وضو
جس میں ڈھل جائیں تو شاید ڈھل سکے
میری آنکھوں، میری گرد آلود آنکھوں کا لہو

When the Heart's Bad Blood

When the heart's bad blood welled up, layer by layer,
in my eyes, there was no other way but to give in
to the counsellor,
and I washed my dust-filled eyes with blood.
And now every object of this sentient world
is so tinted with the blood of my eyes that
bloody is the sun's gold,
bloody the moon's silver
the morning's laughter,
the night's cries—
every tree is a minaret of blood
every flower blood-eyed,
every glance a streak of blood
every reflection blood-soaked.
So long as the blood flows in the vein, its red
is the red of the desire for martyrdom—
pain, rage or sorrow—
and if the flow ceases, it blackens
into mere hate, night, death—
into the mourning shade of every colour.
O my adviser, don't let this happen—
bring me from somewhere a deluge of tears
which may perhaps wash the blood
out of my eyes, my dust-filled eyes.

आरज़ू

मुझे मोजज़ों पे यक़ी नहीं मगर आरज़ू है कि जब क़ज़ा
मुझे बज़्मे दहर से ले चले
तो फिर एक बार ये इज़्न दे
कि लहद से लौट के आसकूँ
तेरे दर पे आके सदा करूँ
तुझे ग़मगुसार की हो तलब तो तेरे हुज़ूर में आ रहूँ
ये न हो तो सूए रहे अदम में फिर एक बार रवाना हूँ

آرزو

مجھے معجزوں پہ یقیں نہیں مگر آرزو ہے کہ جب قضا
مجھے بزمِ دہر سے لے چلے
تو پھر ایک بار یہ اِذن دے
کہ لحد سے لوٹ کے آسکوں
ترے در پہ آ کے صدا کروں
تجھے غمگسار کی ہو طلب تو ترے حضور میں آ رہوں
یہ نہ ہو تو سوئے رہِ عدم میں پھر ایک بار روانہ ہوں

A Wish

I have no faith in miracles
but this wish I do nurture
that when death carries me away from the world,
it should grant me this permission, just once
that I may return from the grave
and, knocking at your door, cry out
if you need a consoler
I'm here.
And if you don't need one,
I may return again to the other world.

सालगिरह

शायर का जश्ने सालगिरह है, शराब ला
मन्सब, ख़िताब, रुतबा उन्हें क्या नहीं मिला
बस नुक़्स है तो इतना कि ममदूह ने कोई
मिस्रा किसी किताब के शायाँ नहीं लिखा

سالگرہ

شاعر کا جشنِ سالگرہ ہے، شراب لا
منصب، خطاب، رتبہ انہیں کیا نہیں ملا
بس نقص ہے تو اتنا کہ ممدوح نے کوئی
مصرع کسی کتاب کے شایاں نہیں لکھا

Anniversary

Bring up some wine, it's a poet's anniversary!
What has not come his way—office, title, status.
There's just this snag though, that the one eulogized
never wrote a single line worthy of any book.

दिन और रात

तीरगी जाल है और भाला है नूर
एक शिकारी है दिन, एक शिकारी है रात
जग समंदर है, जिसमें किनारे से दूर
मछलियों की तरह इब्ने आदम की ज़ात
जग समंदर है, साहिल पे हैं माहीगीर
जाल थामे कोई, कोई भाला लिए
मेरी बारी कब आएगी क्या जानये
दिन के भाले से मुझको करेंगे शिकार
रात के जाल में या करेंगे असीर?

دن اور رات

تیرگی جال ہے اور بھالا ہے نور
اک شکاری ہے دن، اک شکاری ہے رات
جگ سمندر ہے، جس میں کنارے سے دور
مچھلیوں کی طرح ابن آدم کی ذات
جگ سمندر ہے، ساحل پہ ہیں ماہی گیر
جال تھامے کوئی، کوئی بھالا لئے
میری باری کب آئے گی کیا جانیے
دن کے بھالے سے مجھ کو کریں گے شکار
رات کے جال میں یا کریں گے اسیر؟

Day and Night

Darkness a net, and light a spear;
day a hunter, and so is the night.
This world is a sea in which, far from the shore,
live Adam's progeny, like the fish.
The world is a sea on whose shore stand
the fishermen;
some holding nets, others spears.
Who knows when my turn will come
to be hunted down by the day's spear,
or be caught in the night's net?

हमने सब शेर में संवारे थे
हम से जितने सुख़न तुम्हारे थे

रंगो-खुश्बू के, हुस्नो ख़ूबी के
तुमसे थे जितने इस्तेआरे थे

तेरे क़ौलो-क़रार से पहले
अपने कुछ और भी सहारे थे

जब वो लालो गुहर हिसाब किये
जो तेरे ग़म ने दिल पे वारे थे
मेरे दामन में आ गिरे सारे
जितने तश्ते फ़लक में तारे थे
उम्रे जावेद की दुआ करते
फ़ैज़ इतने वो कब हमारे थे

ہم نے سب شعر میں سنوارے تھے
ہم سے جتنے سخن تمھارے تھے

رنگ وخوشبو کے، حسن وخوبی کے
تم سے تھے جتنے استعارے تھے

تیرے قول وقرار سے پہلے
اپنے کچھ اور بھی سہارے تھے

جب وہ لعل وگہر حساب کئے
جو ترے غم نے دل پہ وارے تھے
میرے دامن میں آگرے سارے
جتنے طشتِ فلک میں تارے تھے
عمرِ جاوید کی دعا کرتے
فیض اتنے وہ کب ہمارے تھے

All That You Ever Said to Me

All that you ever said to me
embellished my verse;
all my metaphors were a gift from you—
of colour and fragrance, of beauty and grace.

Indeed, there were other props too for my life,
before your pledges and promises,

while counting all those gems and rubies
your sorrow had bestowed on my heart,

all the stars from the sky's platter
fell into my lap.

Oh, to pray for my eternal life—
when, O Faiz, was she ever so much mine?

मेरे दर्द को जो ज़ुबाँ मिले

مرے درد کو جو زباں ملے

मेरा दर्द नग़मा-ए-बे-सदा
मेरी ज़ात ज़र्रा-ए-बे-निशाँ
मेरे दर्द को जो ज़ुबाँ मिले
मुझे अपना नामो-निशाँ मिले
मेरी ज़ात का जो निशाँ मिले
मुझे राज़े नज़्में जहाँ मिले
जो मुझे ये राज़े-निहाँ मिले
मेरी ख़ामुशी को बयाँ मिले
मुझे कायनात की सरवरी
मुझे दौलते-दो जहाँ मिले

مرا درد نغمۂ بے صدا
مری ذات ذرۂ بے نشاں
مرے درد کو جو زباں ملے
مجھے اپنا نام و نشاں ملے
مری ذات کا جو نشاں ملے
مجھے رازِ نظمِ جہاں ملے
جو مجھے یہ رازِ نہاں ملے
مری خامشی کو بیاں ملے
مجھے کائنات کی سروری
مجھے دولتِ دو جہاں ملے

क़ता

قطعہ

हज़ार दर्द शबे आरज़ू की राह में है
कोई ठिकाना बताओ कि क़ाफ़िला उतरे
क़रीब और भी आओ कि शौक़े दीद मिटे
शराब और पिलाओ कि कुछ नशा उतरे

ہزار درد شبِ آرزو کی راہ میں ہے
کوئی ٹھکانہ بتاؤ کہ قافلہ اترے
قریب اور بھی آؤ کہ شوقِ دید مٹے
شراب اور پلاؤ کہ کچھ نشہ اترے

If Pain Could Speak

My pain, a voiceless song,
my being a nameless mote.
If only my pain could speak,
I'd know who I am.
And if my self could find its essence,
I'd unravel the mystery of this world.
If I could seize this hidden mystery,
my silence would find expression.
Then would I lord it over the universe,
possess all treasures of the two worlds.

Quatrain

A thousand aches in the pathway of the
night of desire.
Show me some shelter so the caravan may
come to rest.
Come closer still to me so that my eager eyes
may be satiated.
Bring me some wine, more wine, so that my
intoxication may wear off.

पाँव से लहू को धो डालो

हम क्या करते किस रह चलते
हर राह में कांटे बिखरे थे
उन रिश्तों के जो छूट गए
उन सदियों के यारानो के
जो इक-इक करके टूट गए
जिस राह चले जिस, सिम्त चले
यूँ पाँव लहूलुहान हुए

सब देखने वाले कहते थे
ये कैसी रीत रचाई है
ये मेहँदी क्यूँ लगाई है
वो कहते थे, क्यूँ क़हत-ए-वफ़ा
का नाहक़ चर्चा करते हो
पाँवों से लहू को धो डालो
ये रातें जब अट जाएँगी
सौ रास्ते इन से फूटेंगे
तुम दिल को संभालो जिसमें अभी
सौ तरह के नश्तर टूटेंगे

پاؤں سے لہو کو دھو ڈالو

ہم کیا کرتے کس رہ چلتے
ہر راہ میں کانٹے بکھرے تھے
اُن رشتوں کے جو چھوٹ گئے
ان صدیوں کے یارانوں کے
جو اک اک کرکے ٹوٹ گئے
جس راہ چلے، جس سمت گئے
یوں پاؤں لہولہان ہوئے

سب دیکھنے والے کہتے تھے
یہ کیسی ریت رچائی ہے
یہ مہندی کیوں لگائی ہے
وہ کہتے تھے، کیوں قحطِ وفا
کا ناحق چرچا کرتے ہو
پاؤں سے لہو کو دھو ڈالو!
یہ راہیں جب اَٹ جائیں گی
سو راستے ان سے پھوٹیں گے
تم دل کو سنبھالو جس میں ابھی
سو طرح کے نشتر ٹوٹیں گے

Wash the Blood off Your Feet

What could we do—where could we go?
Thorns were strewn on every pathway.
Those bonds, now sundered—
Those friendships of centuries
broken, one by one;
whichever way we went, in whatever direction,
the feet were bathed in blood.

Said all those who saw;
what rite is this,
why these hennaed feet?
Said they: why this futile talk
about the drought of loyalty?

Wash the blood off your feet!
When these pathways will be closed,
a hundred new routes will branch out.
You'd better hold your heart
in which a hundred different lancets will break.

ऐ शाम मेहरबाँ हो

ऐ शाम मेहरबाँ हो
ऐ शामे शहरे याराँ
हम पे मेहरबाँ हो
दोज़ख़ी दोपहर सितम की
बे सबब सितम की
दोपहर दर्दो-ग़ैज़ो-ग़म की
बेज़ुबाँ दर्दो-ग़ैज़ो-ग़म की
इस दोज़ख़ी दो पहर के ताज़ियाने
आज तन पर धुनक की सूरत
क़ूस-दर-क़ूस बट गये हैं
ज़ख्म सब खुल गये हैं
दाग़े-जाना था छट गये हैं
तेरे तोशे में कुछ तो होगा
मरहमे-दर्द का दोशाला
तन के उस अंग पर ओढ़ा दे
दर्द सब से सिवा जहाँ हो
ऐ शाम मेहरबाँ हो
ऐ शामे शहरे याराँ
हम पे मेहरबाँ हो
दोज़ख़ी दश्त नफ़रतों के
बेदर्द नफ़रतों के
किरचियाँ दीदाए हसद की
ख़सो ख़ाशाक रंजिशों के

اے شام مہرباں ہو

اے شام مہرباں ہو
اے شامِ شہر یاراں
ہم پہ مہرباں ہو
دوزخی دوپہر ستم کی
بے سبب ستم کی
دوپہر درد و غیظ و غم کی
بے زباں درد و غیض و غم کی
اس دوزخی دوپہر کے تازیانے
آج تن پر دھنک کی صورت
قوس در قوس بٹ گئے ہیں
زخم سب کھُل گئے ہیں
داغ جانا تھا چھٹ گئے ہیں
ترے توشے میں کچھ تو ہوگا
مرہمِ درد کا دوشالہ
تن کے اس انگ پر اڑھا دے
درد سب سے سوا جہاں ہو
اے شام مہرباں ہو
اے شامِ شہرِ یاراں
ہم پہ مہرباں ہو
دوزخی دشت نفرتوں کے
بے درد نفرتوں کے
کرچیاں دیدۂ حسد کی
خس و خاشاک رنجشوں کے

Evening, Be Gracious

O evening, be gracious—
O evening of the city of friends
be gracious to me.
The hellish noon of oppression,
senseless cruelties,
the noon of pain, rage and sorrow,
inarticulate pain, rage and sorrow,
the whiplashes of this demonic noon—
are all, like the rainbow, branded on my body,
arc within arc.

I thought the scars had vanished
but now even the wounds have come alive.
Surely, there must be something
in your sack—a shawl
to cover up that part of the body
where the pain is most intense.
O evening, be gracious—
O evening of the city of friends,
be gracious to me.

The infernal wilderness of scorn,
callous scorn—
splinters of jealous eyes—
the litter of estrangement.

इतनी सुनसान शाहराहें
इतनी गुंजान क़त्लगाहें
जिन से आये हैं हम गुज़र कर
आबला बन के हर क़दम पर
यूँ पाँव कट गये हैं
रस्ते सिमट गये हैं
मख़्मलीं अपने बादलों की
आज पावों तले बिछा दे
शाफ़यी करबे रहरवाँ हो
ऐ शाम मेहरबाँ हो

ऐ मये शबे निगाराँ
ऐ रफ़ीक़े दिलफिगाराँ
ऐ शाम हमज़ुबाँ हो
इस शाम मेहरबाँ हो
ऐ शाम मेहरबाँ हो
ऐ शामे शहरे याराँ
हम पे मेहरबाँ हो

اتنی سنسان شاہراہیں
اتنی گنجان قتل گاہیں
جن سے آئے ہیں ہم گزر کر
آبلہ بن کے ہر قدم پر
یوں پاؤں کٹ گئے ہیں
رستے سمٹ گئے ہیں
مخملیں اپنے بادلوں کی
آج پاؤں تلے بچھا دے
شافئ کربِ رہرواں ہو
اے شام مہرباں ہو

اے مہِ شب نگاراں
اے رفیقِ دلفگاراں
اِس شام ہمزباں ہو
اے شام مہرباں ہو
اے شام مہرباں ہو
اے شام شہر یاراں
ہم پہ مہرباں ہو

Such dreary highways,
so many crowded abattoirs,
through which we have passed,
like blisters at every step.
This is how our feet have been bruised,
pathways have shrunken.
Spread out today your velvety clouds
under our feet;
be the alleviator of suffering wayfarers.

O evening, be gracious.
O moon of the night of love,
O consoler of agonized hearts
commune with us this evening.
O evening, be gracious;
O evening of the city of friends,
be gracious to us.

कुछ इश्क़ किया, कुछ काम किया

वो लोग बहुत ख़ुशक़िस्मत थे
जो इश्क़ को काम समझते थे
या काम से आशिक़ी करते थे
हम जीते जी मसरूफ़ रहे
कुछ इश्क़ किया, कुछ काम किया
काम इश्क़ के आड़े आता रहा
और इश्क़ से काम उलझता रहा
फिर आख़िर तंग आकर हम ने
दोनों को अधूरा छोड़ दिया

کچھ عشق کیا، کچھ کام کیا

وہ لوگ بہت خوش قسمت تھے
جو عشق کو کام سمجھتے تھے
یا کام سے عاشقی کرتے تھے
ہم جیتے جی مصروف رہے
کچھ عشق کیا، کچھ کام کیا
کام عشق کے آڑے آتا رہا
اور عشق سے کام الجھتا رہا
پھر آخر تنگ آ کر ہم نے
دونوں کو ادھورا چھوڑ دیا

Some Love, Some Work

Fortunate indeed were those
who took love as their business
or were in love with whatever they did.
I remained busy all my life—
some love, some work.

Work came in the way of love
and love often impeded work.

Then, finally, in disgust, giving it all up,
I forsook them both, half done.

दिले मन, मुसाफ़िरे मन

मेरे दिल मेरे मुसाफ़िर
हुआ फिर से हुक्म सादिर
के वतन बदर हों हम तुम
दें गली गली सदायें
करें रूख़ नगर नगर का
के सुराग़ कोई पायें
किसी यार-ए-नामाबर का
हर एक अजनबी से पूछें
जो पता था अपने घर का
सर-ए-कू-ए-नाशनायाँ
हमें दिन से रात करना
कभी इस से बात करना
कभी उस से बता करना
तुम्हें क्या कहूँ कि क्या है
शब-ए-ग़म बुरी बला है
हमें ये भी था ग़नीमत
जो कोई शुमार होता
हमें क्या बुरा था मरना
अगर एक बार होता

دلِ من، مُسافرِ من

مرے دل، مرے مسافر
ہوا پھر سے حکم صادر
کہ وطن بدر ہوں ہم تم
دیں گلی گلی صدائیں
کریں رخ نگر نگر کا
کہ سراغ کوئی پائیں
کسی یارِ نامہ بر کا
ہر اک اجنبی سے پوچھیں
جو پتا تھا اپنے گھر کا
سرِ کوئے ناشنایاں
ہمیں دن سے رات کرنا
کبھی اِس سے بات کرنا
کبھی اُس سے بات کرنا
تمہیں کیا کہوں کہ کیا ہے
شبِ غم بری بلا ہے
ہمیں یہ بھی تھا غنیمت
جو کوئی شمار ہوتا
ہمیں کیا برا تھا مرنا
اگر ایک بار ہوتا!

My Heart, My Fellow Traveller

O my heart, my fellow traveller,
once again it's decreed
that we should both be exiled,
let our wailings resound down every lane,
wend our way from town to town
to pick up some friend
with a message from the beloved.

We shall ask every stranger
about our last dwelling.

Standing at the head of some lane where strangers live,
as the day will pass into night,
I'll hold in talk
sometimes this one, sometimes that one.

How shall I tell you
what a curse the night of separation is!
Even dying would be endurable
if one could keep count
of the myriad deaths.

Death would not have mattered to us at all
if it would strike only once!

आज एक हर्फ़ को फिर ढूंढता फिरता है ख़्याल

आज एक हर्फ़ को फिर ढूंढता फिरता है ख़्याल
मधभरा हर्फ़ कोई, ज़हर भरा हर्फ़ कोई
दिल नशीं हर्फ़ कोई, क़हर भरा हर्फ कोई
हर्फ़े उल्फ़त कोई दिलदार नज़र हो जैसे
जिससे मिलती है नज़र बोसए लब की सूरत
इतना रौशन कि सरे मौजए ज़र हो जैसे
सोहबते यार में आग़ाज़े तर्ब की सूरत
हर्फ़े नफ़रत कोई शमशीरे ग़ज़ब हो जैसे
ताअबद शहरे सितम जिससे तबह हो जाएं
इतना तरीक कि शमशान की शब हो जैसे
लब पे लाऊँ तो मेरे होंट सिया हो जाएँ

آج اک حرف کو پھر ڈھونڈتا پھرتا ہے خیال

آج اِک حرف کو پھر ڈھونڈتا پھرتا ہے خیال
مدھ بھرا حرف، زہر بھرا حرف کوئی
دل نشیں حرف کوئی، قہر بھرا حرف کوئی
حرفِ الفت کوئی دلدار نظر ہو جیسے
جس سے ملتی ہے نظر بوسۂ لب کی صورت
اتنا روشن کہ سرِ موجۂ زر ہو جیسے
صحبتِ یار میں آغازِ طرب کی صورت
حرفِ نفرت کوئی شمشیرِ غضب ہو جیسے
تا ابد شہرِ ستم جس سے تبہ ہو جائیں
اتنا تاریک کہ شمشان کی شب ہو جیسے
لب پہ لاؤں تو مرے ہونٹ سیہ ہو جائیں

Today Again is Imagination Seeking a Word

Today again is imagination seeking a word—
some word sweet, or a word soaked in venom.
A word alluring, a word dreadful;
a word of love, enthralling as love's glance
which my eye meets, like the meeting of lips—
effulgent like the crest of a wave of gold.
A word like a prelude to merriment in the
beloved's company,
or a word of hate, like an angry sword
that could destroy all the cities of oppression,
till eternity—
a word as dark as the night in a crematorium,
so dark that if uttered it may blacken the lips.

फूल मुरझा गये सारे

फूल मुरझा गये हैं सारे
थमते नहीं हैं आसमाँ के आँसू
शमएँ बेनूर हो गयी हैं
आईने चूर हो गये हैं
साज़ सब बज के खो गये हैं
पायलें बुझ के सो गयी हैं
और इन बादलों के पीछे
दूर इस रात का दुलारा
दर्द का सितारा
टिमटिमा रहा है
झुनझुना रहा है
मुस्कुरा रहा है

پھول مرجھا گئے سارے

پھول مرجھا گئے ہیں سارے
تھمتے نہیں ہیں آسماں کے آنسو
شمعیں بے نور ہو گئی ہیں
آئینے چور ہو گئے ہیں
ساز سب بج کے کھو گئے ہیں
پایلیں بجھ کے سو گئی ہیں
اور ان بادلوں کے پیچھے
دور اس رات کا دلارا
درد کا ستارا
ٹمٹما رہا ہے
جھنجھنا رہا ہے
مسکرا رہا ہے

All the Flowers Have Withered Away

All the flowers have withered away.
No let up in the flow of the sky's tears.
The lamps have gone lustreless,
the mirrors lie shattered,
and all the orchestras have played
themselves out.
The ankle-bells have done their jingling
and behind the clouds,
far away, this night's beloved,
the star of pain
is twinkling
tinkling
smiling.

कोई आशिक़ किसी महबूबा से

गुलशने याद में गर आज दमे बादे सबा
फिर से चाहे कि गुलअफ़शाँ हो तो हो जाने दो
उम्रे रफ़्ता के किसी ताक़ पे बिसरा हुआ दर्द
फिर से चाहे के फ़रोज़ाँ हो तो हो जाने दो
जैसे बेगाना से अब मिलते हो वैसे ही सही
आओ दो चार घड़ी मेरे मुक़ाबिल बैठो
गरचे मिल बैठेंगे हम तुम तो मुलाक़ात के बाद
अपना एहसासे ज़ियाँ और ज़ियादा होगा
हमसुख़न होंगे जो हम दोनों तो हर बात के बीच
अनकही बात का मौहूम-सा पर्दा होगा
कोई इक़रार न मैं याद दिलाउँगा न तुम
कोई मज़मून वफ़ा का न जफ़ा का होगा

गर्दे अय्याम की तहरीर को धोने के लिए
तुम से गोया हों दमे दीद जो मेरी पल्कें
तुम जो चाहो तो सुनो, और जो न चाहो न सुनो
और जो हर्फ करें मुझसे गुरेज़ाँ आँखें
तुम जो चाहो तो कहो, और जो न चाहो न कहो

کوئی عاشق کسی محبوبہ سے

گلشنِ یاد میں گر آج دمِ بادِ صبا
پھر سے چاہے کہ گل افشاں ہو تو ہو جانے دو
عمرِ رفتہ کے کسی طاق پہ بسرا ہوا درد
پھر سے چاہے کہ فروزاں ہو تو ہو جانے دو
جیسے بیگانہ سے اب ملتے ہو ویسے ہی سہی
آؤ دو چار گھڑی میرے مقابل بیٹھو
گرچہ مل بیٹھیں گے ہم تم تو ملاقات کے بعد
اپنا احساسِ زیاں اور زیادہ ہوگا
ہم سخن ہوں گے جو ہم دونوں تو ہر بات کے بیچ
ان کہی بات کا موہوم سا پردہ ہوگا
کوئی اقرار نہ میں یاد دلاؤں گا نہ تم
کوئی مضمون وفا کا نہ جفا کا ہوگا

گردِ ایام کی تحریر کو دھونے کے لئے
تم سے گویا ہوں دمِ دید جو میرے پلکیں
تم جو چاہو تو سنو، اور جو نہ چاہو نہ سنو
اور جو حرف کریں مجھ سے گریزاں آنکھیں
تم جو چاہو تو کہو، اور جو نہ چاہو نہ کہو

Some Lover to His Beloved

If in memory's garden today, the breeze blows
this moment,
again longing to scatter flowers, then let it be.
If in the niche of days gone by, some forgotten pain
again yearns to be rekindled, then let it be.
Let it be as you'd meet a stranger—
come, just sit there in front of me for a while.
If we'd get together, you and me, then
our sense of loss will grow still more intense;
if we'd lend ourselves to a little talk; between words
there'll hang a fine screen of things left unsaid.
Neither will I remind you of any vow, nor you—
there'll be not a word about commitment
or callousness.

To wipe out the writing of time's dust,
if my eyes speak when I glance at you,
you may listen if you like, or not if you don't.
And if your evasive eyes choose to censure me,
you may say anything you like, or nothing
if you don't.

शायर लोग

हर एक दौर में हम, हर ज़माने में हम
ज़हर पीते रहे गीत गाते रहे
जान देते रहे ज़िन्दगी के लिए
सायते वस्ल की सरखुशी के लिए

दीन व दुनिया की दौलत लुटाते रहे
फ़क़्रो-फ़ाक़ा का तोशा संभाले हुए
जो भी रस्ता चुना, उसपे चलते रहे
मालवाले हक़ारत से तकते रहे
तअन करते रहे, हाथ मलते रहे
हमने उन पर किया हर्फ़े हक़ संगे ज़न
जिनकी हैबत से दुनिया लरज़ती रही
जिन पे आँसू बहाने को कोई न था
अपनी आँख उनके ग़म में बरसती रही
सब से ओझल हुए हुक्मे हाकिम पे हम
क़ैद ख़ाने सहे, ताज़िआने सहे
लोग सुनते रहे साज़े दिल की सदा
अपने नग़मे सलाख़ों से छनते रहे
ख़ूँचकां दहर का ख़ूँचकां आईना
दुःख भरी ख़लक़ा का दुख भरा दिल हैं हम
तबए शायर है जंगगाह अदलो-सितम
मुन्सिफ़े ख़ैरो-शर हक़-व-बातिल हैं हम

شاعر لوگ

ہر اک دور میں، ہر زمانے میں ہم
زہر پیتے رہے، گیت گاتے رہے
جان دیتے رہے زندگی کے لئے
ساعتِ وصل کی سرخوشی کے لئے

دین و دنیا کی دولت لٹاتے رہے
فقر و فاقہ کا توشہ سنبھالے ہوئے
جو بھی رستہ چُنا اس پہ چلتے رہے
مال والے حقارت سے تکتے رہے
طعن کرتے رہے، ہاتھ ملتے رہے
ہم نے اُن پر کیا حرفِ حق سنگ زن
جن کی ہیبت سے دنیا لرزتی رہی
جن پہ آنسو بہانے کو کوئی نہ تھا
اپنی آنکھ ان کے غم میں برستی رہی
سب سے اوجھل ہوئے حکمِ حاکم پہ ہم
قید خانے سہے، تازیانے سہے
لوگ سنتے رہے سازِ دل کی صدا
اپنے نغمے سلاخوں سے چھنتے رہے
خونچکاں دہر کا خونچکاں آئینہ
دکھ بھری خلق کا دکھ بھرا دل ہیں ہم
طبعِ شاعر ہے جنگاہِ عدل و ستم
منصفِ خیر و شر، حق و باطل ہیں ہم

We Poets

We were there—in every age, in every clime,
drinking poison, singing songs;
we kept sacrificing ourselves for life's sake—
for the moment of rapture at love's union.
We kept squandering away our treasure of
spirit and matter,
holding on to our provision of deprivation and hunger.
Whatever path we chose, we stuck to it
even while the affluent kept staring at us disdainfully,
reproachfully, rubbing their palms.
On them we hurled the stone of the word of truth
whose dread kept the world reeling.
And for those who'd none to shed tears over,
our eyes rained tears for their sorrow.
At the ruler's command, we went out of sight,
endured prisons, suffered flogging.
As people listened to the strains of our hearts' cries,
our songs kept filtering through the prison bars.
We are the blood-stained mirrors of this
blood-stained world,
we are the sorrowful heart of anguished humankind.
A poet's temper is to battle against injustice and
tyranny;
we are the arbiters of good and evil, right and wrong.

ये मातमे वक़्त की घड़ी है

ठहर गयी आसमाँ की नदिया
वो जा लगी है उफ़क़ किनारे
उदास रंगों की चाँद नय्या
उतर गये साहिले ज़मीं पर
सभी खेव्वैया
तमाम तारे
उखड़ गयी सांस पत्तियों की
चली गयी ऊँघ में हवाएं
गजर बजा, हुक्म ख़ामुशी का
तो चुप में गुम हो गयीं सदाएँ
सहर की गोरी की छातियों से
ढ़लक गयी तीरगी की चादर
और इस बजाय
बिखर गये उसके तन बदन पर
निरसा तन्हाइयों के साये
और उसको कुछ भी ख़बर नहीं है
किसी को कुछ भी ख़बर नहीं है
कि दिन ढ़ले शहर से निकल कर
किधर को जाने का रूख़ किया था
न कोई जादा, न कोई मंज़िल
किसी मुसाफ़िर को
अब दिमाग़े सफ़र नहीं है
ये वक़्त ज़ंजीर रोज़ो-शब की
कहीं से टूटी हुई कड़ी है

یہ ماتم وقت کی گھڑی ہے

ٹھہر گئی آسماں کی ندیا
وہ جا لگی ہے افق کنارے
اداس رنگوں کی چاند نیا
اتر گئے ساحل زمیں پر
سبھی کھویا
تمام تارے
اکھڑ گئی سانس پتیوں کی
چلی گئی اونگھ میں ہوائیں
گجر بجا حکم خامشی کا
تو چپ میں گم ہو گئیں صدائیں
سحر کی گوری کی چھاتیوں سے
ڈھلک گئی تیرگی کی چادر
اور اس بجائے
بکھر گئے اس کے تن بدن پر
نراس تنہائیوں کے سائے
اور اس کو کچھ بھی خبر نہیں ہے
کسی کو کچھ بھی خبر نہیں ہے
کہ دن ڈھلے شہر سے نکل کر
کدھر کو جانے کا رخ کیا تھا
نہ کوئی جادہ، نہ کوئی منزل
کسی مسافر کو
اب دماغِ سفر نہیں ہے
یہ وقت زنجیر روز و شب کی
کہیں سے ٹوٹی ہوئی کڑی ہے

This is the Moment to Mourn Time

The sky's stream has come to a standstill.
There, the moon's dismal coloured boat
has reached the horizon's fringe.
All the boatmen, all the stars,
have landed on the earth's shore—
The leaves are panting for breath,
the winds have dozed off.
At daybreak, as silence was decreed,
all sounds faded away.
From the breasts of the fair damsel of dawn
has slipped off the shawl of darkness
and instead
are now scattered all over her body—
the shadows of desolate loneliness.
Neither does the dawn know,
nor anybody else, where
at dusk he's set out to go,
leaving the city.
No pathway, no destination;
no traveller has now any inclination for journeying.
This moment, the chain of day and night
seems broken at some point.
This is the moment to mourn time.

ये वक़्त आये तो बे इरादा
कभी कभी मैं भी देखता हूँ
उतार कर ज़ात का लिबादा
कहीं सियाही मलामतों की
कहीं पे गुलबूटे उलफ़तों के
कहीं लकीरें हैं आँसुओं की
कहीं पे ख़ूने जिगर के धब्बे
ये चाक है पंजाए अदू का
ये मुहर है यारे-मेहरबाँ की
ये लाल लबहाए महवशाँ की
ये मरहमत शेख़े बदज़ुबाँ की
ये जामए रोज़ो-शबगज़ीदा
मुझे ये पैराहने दरीदा
अज़ीज़ भी, नापसंद भी है
कभी ये फ़रमाने जोशो-वहशत
कि नोच कर इसको फेंक डालो
कभी ये इसरारे हर्फ़े उल्फ़त
कि चूम कर फिर गले लगा लो

یہ وقت آئے تو بے ارادہ
کبھی کبھی میں بھی دیکھتا ہوں
اُتار کر ذات کا لبادہ
کہیں سیاہی ملامتوں کی
کہیں پہ گُل بوٹے الفتوں کے
کہیں لکیریں ہیں آنسوؤں کی
کہیں پہ خونِ جگر کے دھبے
یہ چاک ہے پنجہ عدو کا
یہ مُہر ہے یار مہرباں کی
یہ لعل لب ہائے مہوشاں کے
یہ مرحمت شیخِ بدزباں کی
یہ جامۂ روز و شب گزیدہ
مجھے یہ پیراہنِ دریدہ
عزیز بھی، ناپسند بھی ہے
کبھی یہ فرمانِ جوشِ وحشت
کہ نوچ کر اس کو پھینک ڈالو
کبھی یہ اصرارِ حرفِ اُلفت
کہ چُوم کر پھر گلے لگا لو

Whenever this moment arrives, I too,
unwittingly, sometimes see,
taking off the garments of self,
somewhere the stains of reproach,
somewhere love's floral embroidery,
somewhere streaks of tears, and
the blots of heart's blood.
Here broke the enemy's claw,
this is the seal of a loving friend,
these the ruddy lips of gracious beloveds,
this the gift of the foul-mouthed priest.

This tattered robe of day and night,
is to me both dear and disdained.
Sometimes, at the behest of frenzy,
I feel like tearing it to shreds
and at times, at love's insistence,
I want to kiss it,
embrace it again.

हम तो मजबूरे वफ़ा हैं

तुझ को कितनों का लहू चाहिए ऐ अर्ज़े वतन
जो तेरे आरिज़े-बेरंग को गुलनार करें
कितनी आहों से कलेजा तेरा ठंडा होगा
कितने आंसू तेरे सहराओं को गुलज़ार करे

तेरे ऐवानों में पुर्ज़े हुए पैमाँ कितने
कितने वादे जो न आसूद-ए-इक़रार हुए
कितनी आँखों को नज़र खा गयी बदख़्वाहों की
ख़्वाब कितने तेरी शहराहों में संगसार हुए

बला कशाने मुहब्बत पे जो हुआ सो हुआ
जो मुझे पे गुज़री मत उससे कहो, हुआ सो हुआ
मुबादा हो कोई ज़ालिम तेरा गिरेबाँ गीर
लहू के दाग़ को दामन से धो, हुआ सो हुआ

हम तो मजबूरे वफ़ा हैं, मगर ऐ जाने जहाँ
अपने उश्शाक़ से ऐसे भी कोई करता है
तेरी महफ़िल को ख़ुदा रखे अबद तक क़ायम
हम तो मेहमाँ हैं घड़ी भर के हमारा क्या है

ہم تو مجبورِ وفا ہیں

تجھ کو کتنوں کا لہو چاہیے اے ارضِ وطن
جو ترے عارضِ بے رنگ کو گلنار کریں
کتنی آہوں سے کلیجہ ترا ٹھنڈا ہوگا
کتنے آنسو ترے صحراؤں کو گلزار کریں

تیرے ایوانوں میں پرزے ہوئے پیماں کتنے
کتنے وعدے جو نہ آسودۂ اقرار ہوئے
کتنی آنکھوں کو نظر کھا گئی بدخواہوں کی
خواب کتنے تری شہ راہوں میں سنگسار ہوئے

بلا کشانِ محبت پہ جو ہوا سو ہوا
جو مجھ پہ گزری مت اس سے کہو، ہوا سو ہوا
مبادا ہو کوئی ظالم ترا گریباں گیر
لہو کے داغ تو دامن سے دھو، ہوا سو ہوا

ہم تو مجبورِ وفا ہیں مگر اے جانِ جہاں
اپنے عشاق سے ایسے بھی کوئی کرتا ہے
تیری محفل کو خدا رکھے ابد تک قائم
ہم تو مہماں ہیں گھڑی بھر کے ہمارا کیا ہے

We are Committed to Loyalty

The blood of how many do you need,
O my motherland,
so that your lustreless cheek may turn crimson?
How many sighs will soothe your heart
—and how many tears make your deserts bloom?

How many pledges lie splintered down your hallways
and how many promises that were never honoured?
How many eyes were cursed by the evil eye
and how many dreams were stoned to death
on your highways?

It matters little what suffering was the lot of love—
don't tell her how much I endured—it's all over now.
Lest some tyrant hold you by the scruff,
let the blood be washed off your hem—
what's done is done.

We're indeed committed to loyalty but, O my love,
should lovers be treated so coldly?
Let God keep your assembly going till eternity—
we're only guests for a moment, we don't
really matter.

पैरिस

दिन ढला कूचओ-बाज़ार में सफ़बस्ता हुई
ज़र्द रू रोशनियाँ
उनमें हर एक के कशकोल से बरसें रिमझिम
इस भरे शहर की नाआसूदगियाँ
दूर पसमंज़रे अफ़लाक में धुंधलाने लगे
अज़मते रफ़्ता के निशाँ
पेशे मंज़र में
किसी साया-ए-दीवार से लिपटा हुआ साया कोई
दूसरे साये की मौहूम सी उम्मीद लिये
रोज़मर्रा की तरह
ज़ेरे लब
शरहे बेदर्दी-ए-अय्याम की तमहीद लिए
और कोई अजनबी
इन रोशनियों सायों से कतराता हुआ
अपने बेख़्वाब शबिस्ताँ की तरफ़ जाता हुआ

پیرس

دن ڈھلا، کوچہ و بازار میں صف بستہ ہوئیں
زرد رُو روشنیاں
ان میں ہر ایک کے کشکول سے برسیں رم جھم
اس بھرے شہر کی ناآسودگیاں
دور پَس منظرِ افلاک میں دھندلانے لگے
عظمتِ رفتہ کے نشاں
پیشِ منظر میں
کسی سایۂ دیوار سے لپٹا ہوا سایہ کوئی
دوسرے سائے کی موہوم سی امید لئے
روزمرہ کی طرح
زیرِ لب
شرحِ بے دردئَ ایّام کی تمہید لئے
اور کوئی اجنبی
ان روشنیوں سایوں سے کتراتا ہوا
اپنے بے خواب شبستاں کی طرف جاتا ہوا

Paris

The day faded away, and down the streets
and alleyways
were arrayed pallid lampposts
from whose bowls rained down
this crowded city's frustrations.
Over there
the vestiges of past glory
began to look hazy against the skyline
and there, in front of the eye,
some shadow embraced a wall's shadow
cherishing the faint hope for another shadow—
an everyday occurrence—
prefaces a mute comment
on the harshness of time—
and some stranger
skirting these lights, these shadows,
presses on towards his dreamless bed-chamber.

क्या करें

मेरी तेरी निगाह में
जो लाख इंतज़ार हैं
जो मेरे तेरे तन-बदन में
लाख दिल फ़िगार हैं
जो मेरी तेरी उंगलियों की बेहिसी से
सब क़लम नज़ार हैं
जो मेरे तेरे शहर की
हर इक गली में
मेरे तेरे नक़्श-ए-पा के बे-निशाँ मज़ार हैं
जो मेरी तेरी रात के
सितारे ज़ख़्म ज़ख़्म हैं
जो मेरी तेरी सुबह के
गुलाब चाक चाक हैं
ये ज़ख़्म सारे बे-दवा
ये चाक सारे बे-रफ़ू
किसी पे राख चाँद की
किसी पे ओस का लहू
ये है भी या नहीं, बता
ये है कि महज़ जाल है
मेरे तुम्हारे अंकबूत-ए-वहम का बुना हुआ
जो है तो इस का क्या करें
नहीं है तो भी क्या करें
बता, बता
बता, बता

کیا کریں

مری تری نگاہ میں
جو لاکھ انتظار ہیں
جو میرے تیرے تن بدن میں
لاکھ دل فگار ہیں
جو میری تیری انگلیوں کی بے حسی سے
سب قلم نزار ہیں
جو میرے تیرے شہر کی
ہر اک گلی میں
میرے تیرے نقشِ پا کے بے نشاں مزار ہیں
جو میری تیری رات کے
ستارے زخم زخم ہیں
جو میری تیری صبح کے
گلاب چاک چاک ہیں
یہ زخم سارے بے دوا
یہ چاک سارے بے رفو
کسی پہ راکھ چاند کی
کسی پہ اوس کا لہو
یہ ہے بھی یا نہیں، بتا
یہ ہے کہ محض جال ہے
مرے تمہارے عنکبوت وہم کا بنا ہوا
جو ہے تو اسکا کیا کریں
نہیں ہے تو بھی کیا کریں
بتا، بتا
بتا، بتا

What Shall We Do?

In your eyes and mine
endless expectations—
in your body and mine
those countless broken hearts—
all the pens paralysed
due to numbness
of your fingers and mine.
Anonymous graves of your footprints and mine
in every lane
of your city and mine.
Those stars wounded, of your night and mine,
those roses ripped apart
of your morning and mine—
these are all wounds beyond healing,
these are tears beyond darning.
On some there's the moon's dust,
on others the dew is wasted.
Whether it is, or isn't, you tell me!
Or is it all a mere web
woven by the spiders of my illusion and yours?
If it is—then what shall we do about it?
And if it isn't, even then, what's to be done?
Tell me, tell me!

अपने इनआमे हुस्न के बदले
हम तही दामनों से क्या लेना
आज फुरक़तज़दों पे लुत्फ़ करो
फिर कभी सब्र आज़मा लेना

اپنے انعام حسن کے بدلے
ہم تہی دامنوں سے کیا لینا
آج فرقت زدوں پہ لطف کرو
پھر کبھی صبر آزما لینا

ढलती है मौजे मय की तरह रात इन दिनों
खुलती है सुबहे गुल की तरह रंगोबू से पुर
वीराँ हैं जाम, पास करो कुछ बहार का
दिल आरज़ू से पुर करो, आँखें लहू से पुर

ڈھلتی ہے موج مے کی طرح رات ان دنوں
کھلتی ہے صبحِ گل کی طرح رنگ و بو سے پر
ویراں ہیں جام، پاس کرو کچھ بہار کا
دل آرزو سے پُر کرو، آنکھیں لہو سے پُر

हमने देखा है मयगुसारों को
पीके और जीके आख़िरश मरते
जो नहीं पीते मौत को उनसे
किस ने देखा है दरगुज़र करते

ہم نے دیکھا ہے مے گساروں کو
پی کے اور جی کے آخرش مرتے
جو نہیں پیتے موت کو ان سے
کس نے دیکھا ہے درگزر کرتے

Quatrains

In recompense for your beauty's largesse
what would you expect of us, the empty-handed?
Why don't you be kind to those afflicted
by separation?
There'll be another time to test their patience.

These days the night ebbs, like the wine's
wave receding.
Dawn breaks like a flower exuding colour
and fragrance.
Empty are the wine-cups; this is no way to welcome
spring—
let the heart be filled with desire, the eyes with blood.

Indeed, I have known drunkards—
die they must, finally, drinking and revelling.
And those teetotallers—has anyone seen death
pass them by?

इश्क़ अपने मुजरिमों को पाबजौलाँ ले चला

दार की रस्सियों के गुलू बंद गर्दन में पहने हुए
गाने वाले शबो-रोज़ गाते रहे
पायलें बेड़ियों की बजाते हुए
नाचने वाले धूमें मचाते रहे
हम न इस सफ में थे और न उस सफ़ में थे
रास्ते में खड़े उनको तकते रहे
रश्क करते रहे
और चुपचाप आँसू बहाते रहे
लौटकर आके देखा तो फूलों का रंग
जो कभी सुर्ख़ था ज़र्द ही ज़र्द है
अपना पहलू टटोला तो ऐसा लगा
दिल जहाँ था वहाँ दर्द ही दर्द है
और गुलू में कभी तौक़ का वाहेमा
कभी पावों में रक्स ज़ंजीर का
और फिर एक दिन इश्क़ उन्हीं की तरह
रसने दर गुलू पाबजौलाँ हमें
इसी क़ाफ़िले में कशाँ ले चला

عشق اپنے مجرموں کو پابجولاں لے چلا

دار کی رسیوں کے گلو بند گردن میں پہنے ہوئے
گانے والے شب و روز گاتے رہے
پائلیں بیڑیوں کی بجاتے ہوئے
ناچنے والے دھومیں مچاتے رہے
ہم نہ اس صف میں تھے اور نہ اس صف میں تھے
راستے میں کھڑے ان کو تکتے رہے
رشک کرتے رہے
اور چپ چاپ آنسو بہاتے رہے
لوٹ کر آ کے دیکھا تو پھولوں کا رنگ
جو کبھی سرخ تھا زرد ہی زرد ہے
اپنا پہلو ٹٹولا تو ایسا لگا
دل جہاں تھا وہاں درد ہی درد ہے
اور گلو میں کبھی طوق کا واہمہ
کبھی پاؤں میں رقص زنجیر کا
اور پھر ایک دن عشق انہیں کی طرح
رسن در گلو، پابجولاں ہمیں
اسی قافلہ میں کشاں لے چلا

Love's Prisoners

Wearing the hangman's noose, like a necklace,
the singers kept on singing day and night,
kept jingling the ankle-bells of their fetters
and the dancers jigged on
riotously.
We who were neither in this camp nor that
just stood by watching them
enviously
shedding silent tears.

Returning, we saw that the crimson
of flowers had turned pale
and on probing within, it seemed
that where the heart once was
now lingered only stabbing pain.
Round our necks the hallucination of a noose,
and on our feet the dance of fetters.

Then came love, one day,
and like the others, enchained, haltered,
we too were dragged into its caravan.

तुम ही कहो क्या करना है

जब दुख की नदिया में हमने
जीवन की नाव डाली थी
था कितना कस बल बाँहों में
लोहू में कितनी लाली थी
यूँ लगता था दो हाथ लगे
और नाओ पूरम पार लगी
ऐसा न हुआ हर धारे में
कुछ अनदेखी मंजधारें थीं
कुछ माझी थे अंजान बहुत
कुछ बेपरखी पतवारें थीं
अब जो भी चाहो छान करो
अब जितने चाहो दोश धरो
नदिया तो वही है, नाव वही
अब तुम ही कहो क्या करना है
अब कैसे पार उतरना है
जब अपनी छाती में हमने
इस देस के घाव देखे थे
था वेदों पर विश्वास बहुत
और याद बहुत से नुस्ख़े थे
यूं लगता था बस-कुछ दिन में
सारी बिपता कट जाएगी
और सब घाव भर जाएंगे
ऐसा न हुआ कि रोग अपने

تم ہی کہو کیا کرنا ہے

جب دکھ کی ندیا میں ہم نے
جیون کی ناؤ ڈالی تھی
تھا کتنا کس بل بانہوں میں
لوہُو میں کتنی لالی تھی
یوں لگتا تھا دو ہاتھ لگے
اور ناؤ پورم پار لگی
ایسا نہ ہوا، ہر دھارے میں
کچھ ان دیکھی منجدھاریں تھیں
کچھ مانجھی تھے انجان بہت
کچھ بے پرکھی پتواریں تھیں
اب جو بھی چاہو چھان کرو
اب جتنے چاہو دوش دھرو
ندیا تو ہی ہے ناؤ وہی
اب تم ہی کہو کیا کرنا ہے
اب کیسے پار اترنا ہے
جب اپنی چھاتی میں ہم نے
اس دیس کے گھاؤ دیکھے تھے
تھا ویدوں پر وشواش بہت
اور یاد بہت سے نسخے تھے
یوں لگتا تھا بس کچھ دن میں
ساری بپتا کٹ جائے گی
اور سب گھاؤ بھر جائیں گے
ایسا نہ ہوا کہ روگ اپنے

What's To Be Done, You Tell

When in the river of pain, we
launched the boat of life,
how much vigour there was in our arms
and how red our blood was.
It seemed that just the push of two hands
and the boat would ferry right across.
But this was not to be—in every current
were unseen whirlpools,
then there were some boatmen—utter novices
and there were also some untried oars.
Now it's for you to probe;
now you may lay any blame at our door—
though it's the same river, the same boat.
Now, you tell us what's to be done,
how are we to get across?
When in our bosom we'd seen the wounds
of this land, we had great faith
in our physicians, and remembered
many a prescription.
It then seemed as though in just a few days
all our troubles would be over—
all wounds healed.
It wasn't that our ailments

कुछ इतने ढ़ेर पुराने थे
वेद उनकी टोह को पा न सके
और टोटके सब बेकार गये
अब जो भी चाहो छान करो
अब जितने चाहे दोश धरो
छाती तो वही है घाव वही
अब तुम ही कहो क्या करना है
ये घाव कैसे भरना है

کچھ اتنے ڈھیر پرانے تھے
ویدان کی ٹوہ کو پا نہ سکے
اور ٹوٹکے سب بیکار گئے
اب جو بھی چاہو چھان کرو
اب جتنے چاہو دوش دھرو
چھاتی تو وہی ہے گھاؤ وہی
اب تم ہی کہو کیا کرنا ہے
یہ گھاؤ کیسے بھرنا ہے

were so chronic, or that our physicians
could not diagnose them—
yet all the curing went in vain.
Now it's for you to probe,
and you may lay all blame at our door.
But it's the same bosom, the same wounds—
now you tell us what's to be done—
how to heal these wounds?

आज शब कोई नहीं है

आज शब दिल के क़रीं कोई नहीं है
आँख से दूर तिलिस्मात के दर वा हैं कई
ख़्वाब दर ख़्वाब महल्लात के दर वा हैं कई
और मकीं कोई नहीं है
कोई नग़मा, कोई ख़ुश्बू, कोई काफ़िर सूरत
कोई उम्मीद, कोई आस, मुसाफिर सूरत
कोई ग़म, कोई कसक,
कोई शक़, कोई यकीं
कोई नहीं है
आज शब दिल के क़रीं कोई नहीं है
तुम अगर हो तो मेरे पास हो
या दूर हो तुम
हर घड़ी साया गरे ख़ातिरे रंजूर हो तुम
और नहीं हो तो कहीं-कोई नहीं, कोई नहीं है
आज शब दिल के क़रीं कोई नहीं है

آج شب کوئی نہیں ہے

آج شب دل کے قریں کوئی نہیں ہے
آنکھ سے دور طلسمات کے در وا ہیں کئی
خواب در خواب محلّات کے در وا ہیں کئی
اور مکیں کوئی نہیں ہے
آج شب دل کے قریں کوئی نہیں ہے
"کوئی نغمہ، کوئی خوشبو، کوئی کافر صورت"
کوئی امید، کوئی آس مسافر صورت
کوئی غم، کوئی کسک، کوئی شک، کوئی یقیں
کوئی نہیں ہے
آج شب دل کے قریں کوئی نہیں ہے
تم اگر ہو، تو مرے پاس ہو یا دور ہو تم
ہر گھڑی سایہ گرِ خاطرِ رنجور ہو تم
اور نہیں ہو تو کہیں ۔۔۔۔ کوئی نہیں، کوئی نہیں ہے
آج شب دل کے قریں کوئی نہیں ہے

Nobody Around Tonight

There's nobody near my heart tonight
Far from the eyes are open many magic portals,
several doors to the palaces of dreams within dreams—
but no inmate.
There's nobody near my heart tonight—
no song, no fragrance, no beloved;
hope adrift like a wayfarer—
no sorrow, no ache, no misgiving, no certitude—
nothing whatsoever.

There's nobody near my heart tonight.
If you're there, whether near me or far away,
then every moment you are a solace for the
stricken heart.
And if you're not anywhere, there's nobody
around, no one—
there's nobody near my heart tonight.

इस वक़्त तो यूं लगता है

इस वक़्त तो यूं लगता है अब कुछ भी नहीं है
महताब, न सूरज, न अंधेरा न सवेरा

आँखों के दरीचों पे किसी हुसन की चिलमन
और दिल की पनाहों में किसी दर्द का डेरा

मुमकिन है कोई वहम था, मुमकिन है सुना हो
गलियों में किसी चाप का एक आख़री फेरा

शाख़ों में ख़्यालों के घने पेड़ की शायद
अब आके करेगा न कोई ख़्वाब बसेरा

एक बैर, न एक महर, न एक रब्त न रिश्ता
तेरा कोई अपना, न पराया कोई मेरा

माना कि ये सुनसान घड़ी सख़्त कड़ी है
लेकिन मेरे दिल, ये तो फ़क़त इक ही घड़ी है
हिम्मत करो, जीने को तो एक उम्र पड़ी है

اس وقت تو یوں لگتا ہے

اس وقت تو یوں لگتا ہے اب کچھ بھی نہیں ہے
مہتاب نہ سُورج، نہ اندھیرا نہ سویرا

آنکھوں کے دریچوں پہ کسی حسن کی چلمن
اور دِل کی پناہوں میں کسی درد کا ڈیرا

ممکن ہے کوئی وہم تھا، ممکن ہے سنا ہو
گلیوں میں کسی چاپ کا اک آخری پھیرا

شاخوں میں خیالوں کے گھنے پیڑ کی شاید
اب آ کے کرے گا نہ کوئی خواب بسیرا

اک بیر، نہ اک مہر، نہ اک ربط نہ رشتہ
تیرا کوئی اپنا، نہ پرایا کوئی میرا

مانا کہ یہ سنسان گھڑی سخت کڑی ہے
لیکن مرے دل یہ تو فقط اک ہی گھڑی ہے
ہمت کرو، جینے کو تو اک عمر پڑی ہے

It Seems at This Moment . . .

It seems at this moment nothing exists—
no moon, no sun, neither darkness nor dawn.

In front of the eyes' windows, some beauty behind
the laced curtain
and in the heart's shelter has come to stay some pain.

Perhaps it was some illusion, or just something
I'd heard talked about
on the street that sound of the last footfalls.

Perhaps in this dense tree, in fancy's boughs,
no dream will ever come to seek refuge.

No estrangement, no affection, no involvement
nobody is yours, for me nobody a stranger.

It's true that this lonesome moment is very cruel
but, O my heart, this is only one such moment.
Take courage, there's all the time to live on.

तुर्क शायर नाज़िम हिकमत के अफ़कार

जीने के लिए मरना
ये कैसी सआदत है
मरने के लिए जीना
ये कैसी हिमाक़त है

अकेले जियो
एक शमशाद तन की तरह
और मिल कर जियो
एक बन की तरह

हमने उम्मीद के सहारे पर
टूट कर यूँही ज़िन्दगी की है
जिस तरह तुम से आशिक़ी की है

ترک شاعر ناظم حکمت کے افکار

جینے کے لئے مرنا
یہ کیسی سعادت ہے
مرنے کے لئے جینا
یہ کیسی حماقت ہے

اکیلے جیو
ایک شمشاد تن کی طرح
اور مل کر جیو
ایک بن کی طرح

ہم نے امید کے سہارے پر
ٹوٹ کر یوں ہی زندگی کی ہے
جس طرح تم سے عاشقی کی ہے

Thoughts of Turkish Poet Nazim Hikmat

To die to live
what good fortune is this.
To live to die
what folly is this.

Walk alone
like an upright box-tree
and live in close togetherness
like the trees in a forest.

Buoyed up on hope,
I've strained my life to its limits—
just as I've been in love with you.

Acknowledgements

I am deeply indebted to Amitendu Bhattacharya, a dear friend and a freelancer, and Revathi Thangavelu, my former colleague, for their invaluable editorial assistance. But, above all, I am grateful to Meru Gokhale, Editorial Director of Vintage India, for encouraging me in completing this project.

A Note on the Author

Courtesy Faiz Foundation Trust, Pakistan (www.faizghar.net)

To Urdu speakers, Faiz Ahmed Faiz needs no introduction. Winner of the Lenin Peace Prize, honoured as a member of the Order of the British Empire, nominated for the Nobel Prize, and awarded Pakistan's highest civilian award, Faiz stands as a colossus of modern Urdu poetry. His poems, with their lyricism and commitment to justice, continue to suture wounds, foment revolutions and inspire ghazal singers.

A Note on the Translator

Shiv K. Kumar has donned many hats and lived many lives: poet, novelist, short-story writer, playwright, translator, academic and critic. He was born in Lahore, where he received his school and college education. He obtained his doctorate in English Literature from the University of Cambridge. Prof. Kumar has published thirteen volumes of poetry, five novels, two collections of short stories and a play. His poems have appeared in several renowned newspapers and journals like the *New York Times*, *Poetry Review* (London), *Western Humanities Review*, among others—and been broadcast on the BBC. In 1978, he was elected a Fellow of the Royal Society of Literature (London). He received the Sahitya Akademi Award in 1987 for his collection of poems *Trapfalls in the Sky*. In 2001, he was awarded the Padma Bhushan for his contribution to literature.